ʹAN THORBURN.

HE AND SHE

Kenneth Barnes, who was born in 1903, was educated at elementary schools, Emanuel School, and
King's College, London. In 1930 he was appointed
senior science master at Bedales, and ten years later
founded a new co-educational boarding school,
Wennington School (now at Wetherby, Yorks). He
and his wife were the principals, until retirement in
1968.

He has given frequent broadcasts, several talks to
sixth-forms on philosophy, taken part in discussions on
sexual problems, psychology and education, and appeared in television programmes on similar subjects.

His statement of faith is to be found in his book
The Creative Imagination (1960), and his educational
philosophy in *The Involved Man* (1969).

He deplores the divisiveness of religion and believes
that the real Christian unity cuts right across sectarian
differences and has little to do with doctrine.

His own interests bridge the 'two cultures', and he
seeks to establish this same bridging throughout education. He sees our world as man-dominated, aggressive
and competitive, and therefore tragically destructive.
It needs, he believes, the full cooperation of women in
changing the spirit and aims of society.

Kenneth Barnes enjoys making things with tools,
painting, photography, acting and producing, sailing
and fell-walking, but at times feels that he would
'swap the lot' for the ability to play a musical instrument. He and his late wife jointly wrote *Sex, Friendship,
and Marriage*; their daughter, who is a doctor, is married, and their son is a university lecturer in education.

KENNETH C. BARNES

HE AND SHE

PENGUIN BOOKS

Penguin Books Ltd, Harmondsworth, Middlesex, England
Penguin Books Inc., 7110 Ambassador Road, Baltimore, Maryland 21207, U.S.A.
Penguin Books Australia Ltd, Ringwood, Victoria, Australia
Penguin Books Canada Ltd, 41 Steelcase Road West, Markham, Ontario, Canada
Penguin Books (N.Z.) Ltd, 182–190 Wairau Road, Auckland 10, New Zealand

—

First published by Darwen Finlayson 1958
Published in Penguin Handbooks 1962
Reprinted with revisions 1962
Reprinted 1963, 1964, 1965, 1967, 1968
Reissued with revisions 1970
Reprinted 1971, 1973, 1975

—

Copyright © Kenneth C. Barnes, 1958, 1962, 1970

—

Made and printed in Great Britain
by C. Nicholls & Company Ltd
Set in Monotype Baskerville

CONTENTS

ACKNOWLEDGEMENT

I could not have written a book on this subject without the continuous help and encouragement of my wife Frances, with whom every idea was discussed and who frequently clarified my statements.

I owe a great deal to the many young men and women, former pupils of mine, who have reported and discussed with me so frankly and helpfully what they have found in their own experience and in the personal and social life of their contemporaries. If this book is to be dedicated to anyone, it should be to these and to the hundreds of others who, as boys and girls growing up in my presence, have given me perhaps my strongest reason for believing in the courage and resilience of humanity.

K.C.B.

I

INTRODUCTION

YET another book about sex? Twenty years ago when, with my wife, I first wrote a book on this subject, it could be fairly said that there were not enough books written for young people in a manner that they could accept. Very many have been written since then and it might seem at first that there was hardly an excuse for another. But it was put strongly to me that a book specially addressed to boys in their middle and late teens and early twenties was necessary. Further, I had become more than ever aware of the unhappy nature of the sexual adventures of boys – or young men – in the late teens, chiefly through reports coming to me from various universities and colleges; and it seemed to me that with every generation new efforts have to be made, new books written, to encourage a better understanding of what is happening and a wiser direction of sexual activity.

But what right has a middle-aged adult to offer advice to the young? If it is thought of simply as advice, then one has little right at all. It is, however, not advice in the old sense. I do not wish to take a moral stand, to say: 'This is right, that is wrong; do the right and you will be happy, do the wrong and you will find yourself in the everlasting bonfire.' Many in the past have taken that point of view, but I doubt if young people have been much helped by it. No, I want to suggest ways by which boys and young men can come to understand what they are doing, understand what happens to them and to the girls they are interested in. Young people have to go their own way, learn their own lessons from their own mistakes. They do not want an adult always at their elbow to take their decisions out of their hands. But perhaps they do need some training or help in

9

the technique of learning lessons from life and in seeing what the facts are from which the lessons can be drawn.

I am a teacher and I know that I do my best work, not when I pump my pupils full of information or tell them exactly what to do, but when I put them in the way of finding out things for themselves, of making their own honest judgements, and of coping with totally unexpected situations. This applies to sexual activity just as much as to any other. The things that happen in real life, especially in intimate relationships with people, are never simple textbook situations. They are always complex, and each situation is always a *new* situation, in which you have to use your own judgement. What I write must therefore be a challenge to develop clear sight and deep thinking.

This does not mean, however, that I shall always be tentative and questioning. There are some actions which, it seems to me, injure the other person in mind and spirit as inevitably as a knife-thrust would injure the body. About these I shall be emphatic. And there are certain basic necessities in a young man's attitude about which I can't find any reason to be hesitant; about these too, I shall be definite.

Much advice given on sexual matters to young people in the past seemed to be given by writers whose very words implied that they thought they knew exactly what they were talking about, that they were outside or had got beyond the conflict themselves, and that they had infallible religious sanction for their advice. Now I want to make it clear that none of us knows all that is to be known about sex, that none of us can claim to be outside it and completely detached, and that many religious judgements have implied a contradiction of true Christianity.

No, we are all made of the same clay, and none of us has the right to speak with superiority. Some of us have indeed experienced fulfilment and lasting happiness in our sexual life and marriage; but we must not claim that this is because we are finer people; we must look into our own upbringing, think of the sort of community we belonged to in our youth, ask what was the quality of the friendships we enjoyed, and then ask how much we owe to these. When we think in this way we find no reason for pride, but only for gratitude. If we offer any of the fruit of our experience to those who are in trouble or bewilderment, it should be with compassion, not with superiority.

Many young people find it difficult to think of their elders as sexual beings, and that is one of the reasons why they do not readily listen to them. 'Dad, you just don't know anything about it!' Almost unconsciously they think of adults, and especially of their parents, as having passed through that stage a long time ago, and therefore not qualified to understand those who are still in it. It should now be said that sexual activity can go on until very late in life and that the secret thoughts of most adults are not very different from those of adolescents. Growing up, becoming mature, and growing old, do not necessarily involve getting rid of the impulses, temptations, dreams, and fantasies, but rather learning how to cope with them so that they do not waste energy and interfere with living. So there is no need for you to think that we older adults are different.

You may want to know what sort of interests I have, what sort of experience or training, that would qualify me to write for young people on this subject. I wouldn't dare to write about this subject if I were not a husband and a father. Also, as I said, I am a teacher, and most of my life I have taught both boys and girls in boarding-schools – schools where one has to get to know one's pupils pretty intimately because one is so deeply responsible for all their personal growing up as well as for their instruction. I've always enjoyed my job, and specially enjoyed every opportunity to get off the platform on which teachers are apt to be put in their pupils' minds. I've always wanted to know what boys and girls really think and feel, and I have therefore tried to create the conditions, inside the classroom and out, in which they feel free to tell me. I'm not easily shocked by what I find in young people, though I find it hard to be patient with cruelty.

I am by training a scientist. I enjoy finding things out, and before making any judgement I want to know as many facts as possible. I do not start from dogmatic or sweeping statements; when I meet these, especially when they concern the nature and conduct of people, my first impulse is to doubt them. I do not mean that they are necessarily untrue, but I will not accept them unquestioningly on someone else's authority, or on the authority of an institution, a party, or a church; if they are true they must be *seen* to be true in my own experience and in the lives of people I know. I don't say that we do not need rules of conduct or that general statements aren't useful, but I do think that we should never apply them unthinkingly to individual cases. Human problems are far more complicated and subtle than anything that we have to deal with in a laboratory. If you apply general ideas insensitively in a laboratory you may retard the progress of science but you will not hurt anybody; but the corresponding way of dealing with human beings may be very cruel. People who are prone to 'moralize' about the conduct of others are often guilty of this sort of cruelty in spite of their supposedly good intentions. It is important to recognize that Jesus was careful not to be forced into this sort of attitude, though his enemies set the trap for him time after time.

So you will find me asking not *how ought people to behave?* but rather *what are men and women like?* and *what happens to them when they behave in certain ways?* You will get little from this book, however, if you think of it as an impersonal statement with which you agree or disagree intellectually. No statement about a deeply human problem can ever be wholly impersonal or dispassionate. There *is* a difference between thinking in a laboratory and thinking about human life. In the laboratory I am outside the test-tube and can be almost wholly detached in thinking about the reaction I am watching. But where human problems are concerned, especially sex, we are all of us, you and I and everyone, *in* the test-tube. Our attitudes are affected by our own experiences and responsibilities. You will have to think of me as one who has a very great deal to do with the growing up of boys and girls between the ages of twelve and eighteen, who watches, with both hope and fear, their leaving school and going out into the world. You will have to use your imagination to be aware of me as alive, faced with all the usual problems of living, sometimes acting clear-sightedly, sometimes muddling through, sometimes doing the effective thing, sometimes making mistakes; but every now and then trying to stand aside and reflect, in order to get a little wisdom that can be applied to my own life or passed on to others. Words written down on a page cannot possibly convey the whole of the thought that is behind them, no matter how carefully they are chosen. Words and statements always originate in living people, they come up out of a complexity of thought and feeling, especially feeling. They mean most when they are said directly by one person to another and when each knows the other well. When I say things to my own pupils it doesn't matter so much that the words are inadequate; they pass directly from one living person to another, and the boy or girl is aware through a great deal of everyday personal contact, of what the words mean *in my experience*. The meaning is much more than the dictionary meanings and their connexion in the sentence. Because you, the reader, are not here beside me, you will have to use your imagination to re-create something of the personal situation from which the thoughts are offered.

Most of the thoughts in this book have been discussed with boys and girls hundreds of times throughout thirty years, in the classroom, in dormitories, on mountains and moors, round meals in camp, and in my own room with old scholars when they come back to report on what they have found in the world.

What sort of boy are you, I wonder? I am trying to speak to every sort, so I have to stretch my imagination a long way.

What sort of literature do you usually read? Comics? Strip-cartoon romances? *Private Eye*? *Playboy*? *Reveille*?

The News of the World? Men Only? If you read any of these
what do you think you are looking for in them? What do
your eyes move towards as you flick over the pages? I
wonder whether you find the love-life of film stars really
interesting and what sort of feelings you have as you look at
the nearly naked women's bodies. Do these things really *get*
you, or can you, even though you can't keep your eyes
away, look at them with a certain amount of amused detachment? Are you really interested in a drawing of a
sporty-type looking goggle-eyed at a nearly naked, big-
breasted, heavily lipsticked girl?

It may be that you are one of those boys who will read
anything, whatever the bookstall offers you in an idle
moment, as well as your 'set-books' and any novel, good or
bad, that you can get from the local library. If this is so, are
you beginning to get an ability to discriminate – to distinguish between the good and the bad, the book that is
sincerely written and the one that is just a pot-boiler
written to a recipe?

What sort of films do you prefer? Westerns, escape
stories, crime, romance? Musicals, with noisy females, half-
dressed, crooning and kicking their long bare legs? Do you
like seeing women knocked about by tough-looking men,
and does it stir in you the impulse to do likewise? Are you
able to enjoy a film when it hasn't got a love-element in it?
Or do you hate it because it has? What do you feel like
during these close-up kisses, long-drawn-out and well-
worked-round? Are you beginning to discriminate between
good films and poor films, and do you ever listen to *The
Critics?* Why do you go to films, anyway, and what do you
feel like when you come out into the street after it's all over?

Have you ever thought? That must seem a strange question, but it is nevertheless true that many people hardly
think at all – not in a logical way. They only see a succession
of images, or feel a series of feelings, without reflecting upon
what they see or feel. Do you just go with the crowd? Do
you feel clever if you can say something that every one of
your pals approves, or do you sometimes feel compelled to

disagree? Can you stand outside the crowd or do you feel that you have to go with it? Can you sometimes stand aside and ask occasionally: *What does it all mean, what am I looking for, why am I here?*

If you have read as far as this you might pause now and think for a moment of the money that is made out of you, think of the vast flood of print, the thousands of miles of film, put out to satisfy your demands and the demands of the vast majority of people – for you are not alone in your interests. Somewhere a great army of people is cashing in on the racket of satisfying your demands. Can you imagine how often, among the film producers and the magazine editors, many of whom are very intelligent people, the remark is heard: 'If we're going to make money we've got to give the mugs what they want!' *Are* we a lot of mugs; *need* we be? Here we are in a civilization that has gone further ahead than we ever dared to dream in its scientific and technical achievement. Production of every sort goes steadily upwards; whole forests of timber disappear into the paper-making machines, the relatively new plastics industry increases at a tremendous rate, more and more steel and aluminium are poured into motor works, electronic valves are produced in endless variety and by the million – and to a very large extent this is to provide us with *amusement*. Newspapers, magazines, books, films, records, radio, television, cars, caravans.

Surely we ought to be the freest, richest, most satisfied people that ever lived? Are we?

Here is another set of questions. Do your activities satisfy you? What does your reading do for you – does it answer your questions? What questions? Do you question life and its experiences? Here's a question that is a bit of a facer for some: *Can you bear to be alone?* If you can't, why not? Do you feel that you must have company, you can't bear isolation? Perhaps you have begun to feel that eventually you will get the companionship you most need from a girl. Now what do you think about girls? How many do you know? Perhaps you are at a stage when you 'have no use for them'. Perhaps you pretend one thing and do another. Among your friends you express a contempt for girls' lack of knowledge of technical and mechanical things, cars, planes, etc. Yet you whistle at them, and are excited in their presence. And privately, possibly publicly, when 'The Boys' are around, you are very interested in the girls' bodies. Have you ever thought that any of these girls might be interesting persons, gentle, understanding, kind, perhaps even comforting when you need that sort of thing? Or are you still in the mood when they seem noisy, crude creatures, yelling back cheeky remarks at street corners? You might of course be one of those boys who keep in with the crowd in public, but in your secret thoughts cherish a dream.

If you are still in your early teens, probably what you want to know is how a girl's body is made, and how it is different from yours; you want to know how your own sex organs work, and how a baby grows inside a woman's body. This book will tell you a good deal about all that and there are books that will tell you more. But if you are older, your thoughts when alone are probably concerned more with how to reconcile your own sexual urges with your social life and the demands of society. Unless you are an unusual person, or not growing up as fast as others, you will be aware all the time of the intrusion of sexual ideas, dreams, and impulses upon everything else you wish to do. When you are engaged in study sexual thoughts will squeeze their way in and destroy your concentration. One of the greatest difficulties for serious young people arises from the fact that during that period of life when sexual urges are strongest and sexual thoughts most insistent, they are expected to give all their minds to study – to sit for hours motionless in chairs devoting their whole thought to things that have nothing to do with themselves. For this and other reasons the student world is a strange and abnormal world, and I have devoted a chapter to it.

The appeal of sex is enormously strong. A casual glance at advertisements will show that. You can sell anything by sex appeal, not only underclothing, toothpaste, and cosmetics. You can use a nearly naked girl's body not only to sell a new bra, but steel tubes and nuts and bolts. But sex is important at a much deeper level. I have to be careful at this point not to give support to the popular attitude that the first thing in life is to be sexually satisfied and that only when that has happened can you be expected to get on with other things. That is not true and the result of believing it will be that you will never be satisfied. Many people have achieved a joyful and deeply satisfying life without sex experience; that is just a plain undeniable fact. Yet for most of us, to be sexually satisfied in a joyful way – a way that carries no sense of guilt – does make a very great difference to life. It is one of those experiences that show us really what it is to be *set free*. The man or woman who knows this joy and can contrast it with the longing and frustration – and perhaps guilt – that preceded it, knows what freedom means. It does not mean the possibility of following every whim or desire without restriction; it is rather the opening up of a whole new world of experience. It is not the only way to this sort of freedom, for, as I have said, many people have achieved fulfilment without sex experience, but it is the way for most people.

But not only at the deep level does sex offer enjoyment. What about leg-shows, pin-ups, hot films? Obviously they offer enjoyment, but of what sort? Isn't it nearly always an excitement that has a furtive, guilty quality about it? When a group of youngsters gets amusement out of these things, isn't the amusement artificially pepped-up by the awareness that it is a sort of *defiance*, a defiance of what are regarded as good standards, a defiance of the people who want you to be better than you are, and possibly a defiance of something in yourself? When a boy laughs and sniggers, his enjoyment is not really *free*, because underlying it there is a feeling, however slight, of shame. There is a different quality of enjoyment to be found in sex experience when there is no shame to spoil it, when you know without any doubt that it is *good*. Those who go in for the sniggering, goggle-eyed enjoyment are apt to think of the other sort of enjoyment as too solemn, so solemn as to take away all the fun. Admittedly, many heavy-handed adults in the past have made it seem so, but my attitude has nothing in common with theirs. I don't want to take away any of the fun, the gaiety, and the laughter; indeed in comparison with what I know to be possible I consider what is offered to the public as a substitute is a very poor one.

You will find from your reading of this book that I am ready to admit that we *all* of us, teachers or pupils, responsible thoughtful people or hooligans, parsons or barrowboys, share the same sexual interests. The attention of all of us is caught by nakedness or bodies partly revealed. We are all interested in 'love' and in what men and women do in private, in our own bodies and their strange demands. Exactly the same sort of interests and sources of enjoyment are present both in a good sexual experience and a bad one; it is the quality of the interest that is different, and the way it is related to one's whole life. The good experience leaves no guilt; it is supremely satisfying; it can be thought of afterwards with a sensual relish, yet as having given something deep and lasting to one's life. Good sexual experience gives a man or woman a great sense of being 'at home in the world', at home in a *good* world. The bad experience does not bring lasting satisfaction, or the sense of having been given something big and significant; it often results in a craving for something more artificially stimulated, which in turn must prove unsatisfying.

If you think of sexual experience as isolated experience, something separate and on its own, a mere means of enjoyment, you will spoil it and make certain of dissatisfaction. It is basically part of the whole pattern of events concerned with mating, child-bearing, family life, and education, and because these events deeply concern us as *human* beings, sexual experience must be part of the business of getting to know each other as *persons*. But because sexual impulses are very strong in themselves, there has always been a strong tendency to indulge them as though they had no connexion with family life or with getting to know each other. This

tendency has been enormously exaggerated by the discovery
that there is money to be made out of it, through entertainment and prostitution.

What I maintain in this book is that the most lasting
satisfaction from sex comes when we put sex back where it
belongs, when we think of it as something that happens
between people who really care for each other, who increasingly enjoy each other, who take responsibility for each
other and for the outcome of their love.

Does this mean that you must all follow the conventional
moral code?

2

THE SEX ORGANS

THERE are now many books written for young people giving all the facts they ought to know about their own bodies and their sex organs. But you may not have come across one of these books and I therefore include some chapters about these topics. (Chapters 2, 3, and 4.)

First I must outline how male and female together provide what is necessary for the birth of young. The female produces *ova* (*ovum* is Latin for egg), one or two a month, from her ovaries, which are two oval-shaped organs in the lower part of the abdomen. These ova are extremely small – too small to be seen – and if they are not fertilized they pass out of the body unnoticed. The male prod·ces millions of even smaller cells, only just large enough to be seen under the high power of an ordinary microscope, and during the orgasm these are ejected from the penis into the vagina of the female. Only one of the millions of sperm cells, as they are called, is required to fertilize an egg. If the egg is fertilized it burrows into the surface of the womb and begins to grow into a baby, which after nine months will be ready for birth. This process will be described in greater detail later.

Now for the details of a woman's reproductive organs. First look at the side view as it might be imagined if the right-hand half of the body were removed. (Fig. 1.) The cleft between the legs has two sets of lips, or *labia*, the outer ones which usually close the opening being rounded and firm, the inner ones looser and less shaped. The whole area is the *vulva* and the inner space the *vestibule*. Into it come two tubes, the one in front from the bladder and used to discharge urine, the other the vagina, leading from the womb and of a size to receive the penis during intercourse. The third opening is the anus; this is outside and behind the vulva. All this part of the body is surrounded by a ring of bone called the pelvis; this spreads out from the spine at the back into the two broad blades of bone under the hips and joins up in the bridge in front called the *symphysis pubis*. A woman's pelvis is broader than a man's because a baby may have to pass through the opening, but the essential shape is the same.

There is a very small organ in the front of the vulva where the inner labia joins. It is called the clitoris and it is like the tip of a minute penis; indeed it is what corresponds in the woman's body to the penis in a man's. No tube passes through it and its only value is that during sexual activity it becomes, like the penis, very sensitive and excitable. When a woman is really prepared for intercourse the clitoris becomes a little enlarged and more prominent, a process corresponding to the erection of the penis. At the same time the tissue round the vagina becomes distended with blood, this tending to open the vagina and make the insertion of the penis easier. Just inside the opening of the vagina there are some glands – Bartholin's glands – which produce a liquid when the woman is sexually aroused, and this liquid lubricates the movement of the penis in and out of the vagina.

The vagina must not be thought of as an open tube; normally it is flattened by the pressure of the other organs and tissues. In a virgin, the opening into the vulva is partly covered by skin forming the *hymen*. As will be explained later this is broken by intercourse and in some instances it is negligible to begin with. Now we must consider the inner organs. The vagina is about three or four inches long. This may seem small in relation to the size of an erect penis, but the wall is made of very elastic tissue, capable of a great deal of stretching. The womb, or uterus, is at the inner end and the mouth of the womb projects into the vagina like a knob, with a very small hole in it. As you can see from the diagram, the womb is of about the same length as the vagina; it has a thick wall and a narrow cavity in it. Two tubes branch out like horns from its inner end, and these are called the Fallopian tubes. If the womb and its attached organs are spread out they look as they are shown in Fig. 2, and you can see that the two tubes have fringed ends which seem to grasp the ovaries – these are oval lumps a little over an inch long.

The ovaries are similar to a man's testicles in size and shape but have a different structure inside. They are full of tiny cavities; these are already present when a girl baby is born, many thousands of them, and are called Graafian follicles. It is in these that the ova (eggs) develop but it is in a sense true to say that a girl has all her eggs when she is born; they only have to mature. This implies that it is very unlikely that anything she experiences as she grows up will affect the qualities she will pass on to her children. She will not give her daughter red hair by living on a diet of carrots or make her a platinum blonde by going to see a film star every week at the cinema. When a girl reaches puberty at about twelve some of these follicles begin to swell and move towards the outside of the ovary. Eventually they enlarge until about half an inch in diameter, filled with liquid under increasing pressure. Attached to one side of the cavity there is an ovum. This egg cell, when it is ready, is of such small size that eight of them could be put side by side in a millimetre, or two hundred in an inch. It is protected while still in the follicle by a ring of much smaller cells. At the right time in the month the follicle reaches the outside of the ovary, making a swelling that eventually bursts and shoots out the egg. There is a slow movement of lymph, the colourless liquid that keeps all the organs moist, passing down the Fallopian tubes into the uterus, and the ovum is carried by this into the fringed ends and through the tube. It is here that it may meet sperm cells if there has been sexual intercourse, and fertilization may thus occur in the tube while the ovum is on its way to the uterus. The tubes are very folded and rough inside, so the journey takes several days. I shall describe the development of the fertilized egg in another chapter.

The time at which the ovum is set free from the follicle is

a definite point in the menstrual or oestrus cycle, as it is called, and something must now be said about this. After she reaches puberty a girl begins to lose blood from her vagina during a few days in each month. The 'month' may be, say, 26 or 28 days or a similar period, varying a little from girl to girl. This is the process of menstruation, and the 'cycle' is the round-and-round succession of events inside the girl's body of which the loss of blood is a part. The process is all controlled by the pituitary, a gland in the brain, which plays a dominant part in the control of our bodily processes, especially through its front or anterior lobe. It has been likened to the conductor of an orchestra, who decides when the various instruments should come in. If the anterior pituitary gland is damaged or diseased, great changes take place – producing a giant or a dwarfed body, an ugly lack of proportion in bones, and many other alterations. Fortunately the pituitary is a very reliable conductor and abnormalities are rare. It does its job, an extremely complicated one, with amazing regularity. In the woman it sends a chemical, called a hormone, round in the blood to stimulate the follicles to swell and get ready to burst. Another hormone from this gland stimulates the empty follicle, after the departure of the ovum, to fill up with a mass of cells called the *corpus luteum*. This in turn produces yet another hormone which causes the surface of the uterus to get ready for a fertilized ovum to be planted on it. This hormone is called *progesterone*, a portmanteau word meaning get-ready-for-gestation. This is an over-simplified account of what is in fact a very complicated chemical adjustment.

If a fertilized ovum is to begin to grow in the inner surface of the uterus it must have a rich blood supply and a spongy layer of tissue to sink into. The hormone makes the inner surface grow rapidly so that it acquires a new layer perhaps a quarter of an inch in thickness. But what if the ovum is not fertilized? For reasons I will explain later, it won't stick to the surface and will pass out of the vagina or break up. The uterus has prepared itself for nothing. Then it has to get rid of the new surface and have a rest before starting the process all over again. The cells on the surface break away and pass out of the body together with a certain amount of blood. Some girls do not lose much blood and the 'period' lasts only two or three days; others lose more and it takes as long as a week to diminish to nothing. There is usually a certain amount of lassitude during menstruation, but the modern girl is not encouraged to coddle herself. She usually excuses herself only from the vigorous activities that would cause discomfort.

The Male Sex Organs

Since this book is for boys and young men I need hardly describe the external appearance of the penis and testicles. But there are some things to be explained and one of these is circumcision, which puzzles and worries some boys. Circumcision is the cutting off of the loose skin covering the end or *glans* of the penis. This skin is called the *prepuce* or *foreskin*. The operation is often done to boy babies fairly soon after birth, but it can be done at any later stage and even in adulthood. It is a very ancient practice and often referred to in the Bible; all orthodox Jews practise it. The historical origins of the practice are very obscure. It appeared independently in widely separated parts of the world, and possibly primitive hygiene had something to do with it, arising from the inflammation that sometimes occurs under the foreskin of uncircumcised boys. But certainly it became of great ritual significance, in some tribes an initiation into manhood and carried out in the teens, and among the Jews a symbol of deep religious importance. The story of Abraham and his covenant with God suggests that circumcision became a sign that he and his people had embraced a religion that abhorred the practice of child sacrifice so widespread among other semitic nations, and circumcision may have been a ritual substitution for it. It is frequently carried out today for purely practical reasons, perhaps chiefly the hygienic one given above. But it is not necessary

26

even for this, because a tight foreskin, that cannot be pulled right back to uncover the end of the penis so that it can be washed, can be stretched by a doctor until this is easily possible. Cleanliness is very important, and boys and men should pay special attention to it. The ridge behind the glans produces a fatty material, which gives rise to an unpleasant smell if it is not frequently washed away. Some boys worry when a mischief-maker tells them that circumcision will prevent their having sexual intercourse. It has no effect whatever on a man's ability to have satisfying sex intercourse.

The penis consists mainly of three cylinders of spongy tissue held together by a fibrous envelope and skin. The smaller cylinder running up the underside of the penis carries the tube – *urethra* – through which urine or seminal fluid is passed out. It is the spongy nature of these cylinders that makes erection possible. There is a nerve that runs from near the base of the spine into the tissue of the penis; and when a message comes along this nerve the cavities in the spongy tissue open up to receive blood. At the same time the flow of blood away from the penis through veins is partly restricted, and the pressure of the blood pumped into the penis by the heart causes it to swell up and become firm.

The sac or *scrotum* in which the testicles hang corresponds to the outer lips of the vulva in a woman, and the penis to the clitoris much enlarged. The testicles, or *testes*, do not have the same sort of cavities as an ovary, but long cavities running the whole width of the testes and opening into a space on one side. In each of these cavities, of which there are about 800, there is a tiny, much-folded tube, which if unravelled and stretched out would be about two feet long. In one testis, therefore, there must be about 1,600 feet of this tubing and in the two testes together well over half-a-mile. In each of the *seminiferous tubules* there is a lining of cells busily producing sperm cells. These sperm cells are held in clusters with their tails outward, attached to the lining, until they are ready to be set free. Then they pass into the space at the side of the testis and into another

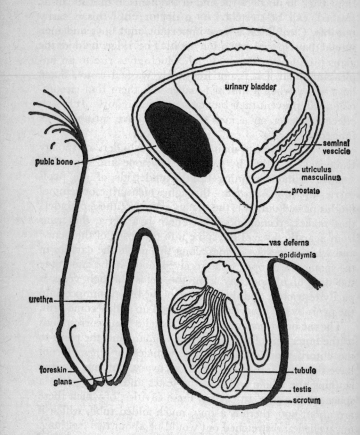

Fig. 3. Male Sex Organs

seemingly tangled mass of tubing, the *epididymis*. This can be easily felt as a bunchy mass on one side of each testis. From the epididymis the tube called the *vas deferens* ('carrying-away-tube') leads to the penis. Before the vas deferens joins the urethra it meets the opening of the seminal vesicle

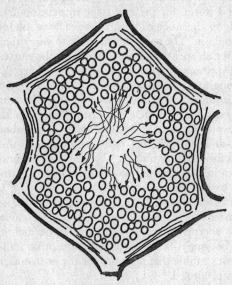

Fig. 4. Section of Seminiferous Tubule
showing sperm cells still attached to the layer of cells
from which they were formed

and the prostate gland and another smaller gland – Cowper's gland. When the orgasm takes place all the vessels and glands contract and the seminal fluid that comes out of the penis is a mixture of sperm cells with liquids produced by the glands.

The sperm cells are not active until they are mixed with these liquids. They can wait in the epididymis for many days in an inactive condition, but when made active by the

mixture of liquids they begin to move by lashing with their
tails. Spermatozoa are much smaller than ova. They have
to travel perhaps 30,000 times their own length and they
must travel light. Both ova and sperms are single cells, each
with a nucleus containing all the material for passing on
inheritable characteristics. The egg needs also some nourishment, food stores, for the first stage in development if it is
fertilized; so the nucleus is surrounded by a blob of jelly-
like protoplasm. The sperm needs only to carry the inheritance material, so it has little other than the nucleus in its
head and presumably just enough 'fuel' to keep it moving
long enough. Nevertheless it is surprising how long a
spermatozoon can keep going and how fast it can travel,
relatively speaking. Stretched out head to tail five thousand
of them would occupy an inch, yet they travel about three
inches in an hour, and they can remain alive in the vagina
or uterus for about two days. The amount of seminal fluid
driven out in one orgasm, about a teaspoonful, can contain
as many as 250,000,000 sperms. Nature is trying to make
sure that at least one of them will get to its destination! It is
indeed necessary, for a man who only produced, say,
5,000,000 sperms in one orgasm would be definitely less
likely to become a father. It is, of course, that half-mile of
seminiferous tubule that accounts for the enormous number
of sperms produced.

It should be said here that there is no truth in the story
that it is good for health to get rid of the sperm cells you
produce and that therefore you should either masturbate or
have sexual intercourse. The sex organs do not suffer
through not being able to discharge the fluid. The liquids
and the sperm cells are simply reabsorbed, digested back
into the tissues of the body. But the ceaseless activity of the
organs, especially in youth, and the urgency of sex feeling,
tend to cause a tension that leads to 'wet dreams', the
spilling of fluid in sleep.

It is unfortunate that young people cannot help hearing
about abnormalities, and sometimes they become unduly

disturbed by what they hear. One of the abnormalities is that concerning change of sex. To most boys and girls it is fascinating, yet horrifying. They ask if it could happen to them. First, it is important to realize that you rarely hear the whole truth from newspaper accounts, and often the accounts are distorted versions of what has really happened. Secondly, you should realize that these things are made headline news because they appeal to the morbid interests of the public (we all have these interests in some measure!) and thus they are made to seem more frightening and more frequent than they really are.

It is an anatomical fact that we *all* have some of the characteristics and the organs of the opposite sex. The clitoris is an example. Another is the extremely small pouch near the prostate gland called the *utriculus masculinus*, or little male womb. It is in fact a rudimentary womb, as small in comparison with a real womb as a clitoris is compared with a penis. Also, a boy is born with nipples in the same place as a girl has them, and occasionally a swelling begins in adolescence as though the boy were about to have breasts. If the appropriate hormone were put into his body he would actually develop breasts. Such possibilities arise from the fact that a baby, some time before it is born, has the rudiments of the organs of *both* sexes. If it is to be a boy the male sex organs will become larger and the female ones will remain rudiments; if it is to be a girl the opposite will happen. But there are rare occasions when nature does not do the job properly; the baby may be born appearing outwardly to be female but having under the surface moderately developed male sex organs. This is not realized at first but becomes more obvious perhaps in the teens. I have said that these occurrences are rare. They are so rare that you need not fear such an abnormality in yourself; there are many other things in life that are much more to be feared! More frequently there are little imperfections, for instance a penis that is open underneath. These little untidinesses of nature can be dealt with effectively by surgery.

Not only do all of us have a little of the opposite sex in our bodies but we have the same in our personalities. No one is completely masculine; all men have some of the feminine in them, some more, some less. This is good, for it helps a man to understand the opposite sex. A completely masculine man would not make a good husband.

If the sex organs are removed by surgical operation it will leave a man much more under the control of the hidden female tendencies in him. The removal of the testes, in the operation known as castration, is regularly performed on male farm animals to make them less active and put on more flesh; they become more like the female. When this is done to boys they become eunuchs, and they too are fat and heavy. You will often read of eunuchs in the history and stories of the East; they were usually slaves castrated when young and later made the guardians of the ruler's women-folk, because they could not themselves interfere sexually with the women. A castrated boy does not put on hair when he reaches his teens and his voice does not break and for this reason castration was practised until the nineteenth century in Italy to provide choir boys who would keep their pure soprano voices. Most normal men feel anger and disgust at the thought of this being done to a boy, no matter what the purpose may be. Obviously the boys can never become fathers, nor satisfactory husbands.

You will probably hear also about impotence. Impotence is the inability to carry out the sex act, and the term usually applies only to a man. Most often it is because the man's penis will not become erect or will not remain erect. It should be known that when this happens it is not necessarily because there is anything physically wrong; it is usually because for some reason the man is anxious, afraid, guilty, or in some other disturbed condition of mind that prevents him from being caught up in the enjoyment of mating. He may have no idea of what is wrong in his mind, and the help of a doctor who understands the mental side of sex is usually necessary. The corresponding condition in women is frigidity. A frigid woman either cannot be roused sexually or suffers from a muscular spasm that keeps the vagina closed. She too may need medical help. But no young man should ever charge a girl with being frigid just because she does not readily respond to sexual advances. A girl may hold herself back from all invitations to flirting and petting, and even seem largely uninterested, yet be able to give herself wholeheartedly to the man she eventually comes to love.

Then there is disease. Venereal disease was forced on my attention when I was an adolescent, because it spread rapidly among soldiers during the first world war and news filtered through of huge camps of infected soldiers, men set apart by the army authorities in an attempt to control the spread of the disease. The men often brought the disease home, and soon we were told that, on an average, every tenth house was infected. With the coming of new drugs, and especially the development of penicillin treatment during the second world war, it seemed that the disease would be conquered, perhaps banished from human experience. This was too optimistic a hope. Resistant strains of both syphilis and gonorrhoea have appeared, and these diseases have rapidly extended, especially among teenagers. Research workers attempt to keep pace with the new strains of germs by making new chemical derivatives of the drugs; but the principal problem is to make the public fully informed and to persuade people to report any symptoms at once to a doctor or a clinic – at which, by the way, secrecy is always guaranteed.

I do not propose to deal extensively with the subject in this book; there is plenty of information available now for those who need it, but I must say enough to help readers to recognize whether they do need more information and to encourage them to get it. Syphilis is contracted only by contact with another person who is suffering from it; the germ is transmitted during sexual intercourse. There are some instances of people being infected by kissing another person who has an infected sore on the lip; but the disease cannot be caught by anything other than contact, *not* from towels, for instance. The germ dies very quickly when it is deprived of the warmth of the body. You cannot catch any disease by handling your penis. You may get irritation and inflammation if you do not wash thoroughly, but this will not be any different from inflammation elsewhere on your body; it should be reported at once and can be quickly cleared up. A tight foreskin that prevents washing underneath should be reported to the doctor. These are simply routine matters; there need be no shame about them.

Syphilis begins with a sore on the sex organ and this sore may fairly soon disappear. The spirochaete, as the germ is called, will then be wandering through the body if there has been no medical treatment. As a result there will be a second stage in which sores break out on other parts of the body, for instance the lips. These too will eventually disappear, even if there is no treatment, but this does not mean cure. A third stage will be established in which the spirochaetes begin to colonize interior organs or invade the nervous system, causing disorders of muscular control, paralysis, and perhaps eventually insanity. The disease can be arrested, at this or any other stage, by medical treatment. Anyone who has ever been infected and who contemplates marriage should undergo a Wasserman test to make sure that there is no trace in his body; he should be honest about it with the woman he intends to marry. If the germ is present in the third stage, he cannot infect his wife, but he may become a physical wreck – perhaps years afterwards – and a burden to her. An infected woman can pass the disease on to her child in the womb, even during the third stage, for it is one of the germs that can pass across the placental barrier. In that event the baby acquires congenital syphilis and rarely survives.

Much of the spread of syphilis has been due to prostitutes, the women who make a living by giving themselves to men for payment. If a prostitute is infected by one of the men she has intercourse with, she may pass it on to most of the men who afterwards come to her, and the spread will be extremely rapid.

The other principal disease is gonorrhoea. This restricts itself to the passages in the organs themselves, causing inflammation and catarrh. It is caught in the same way as syphilis. It is not so terrible to the persons themselves, but its worst danger is that the baby of a woman infected by the disease may be made blind by the germs from the vagina reaching its eyes. The disease should be medically treated immediately. It is quickly cured by penicillin.

There are less well-known diseases of the sex organs and urinary passages, such as *non-specific urethritis;* but all that remains for me to say now is that while it is foolish to risk the contagion of venereal disease, no one should be held back by embarrassment or shame from seeking professional medical advice if there are any symptoms that could possibly indicate infection. In so far as it is possible it should be thought of just like any other disease, and everyone owes it to himself and to the community to help in eradicating it.

It is in a way sad that a book of this sort should have to include these references to disease, and disease that is so revolting. The sex organs themselves, looked at from the point of view of structure and physiology, are fascinating and wonderful; the disease that attacks them seems by contrast the more horrible. This contrast appears throughout sexual activity, the contrast between its possible beauty and its possible degradation. It must, however, be pointed out that venereal diseases are not necessarily associated with immorality. They are not a punishment for sin, as the old moralists used to say. There was no syphilis in Europe until the sailors of Columbus's time brought it back with them from the Caribbean, and there may come a time soon when it will be exceedingly rare, no matter how people behave. That does not mean that bad behaviour will not bring consequences; it will, but not the sort that can be cured by drugs!

3

PREGNANCY AND BIRTH

WHEN a man is married and his wife is beginning to bear a child, the development of the tiny embryo in her womb and all the other things that happen in her body can become of intense interest to him. To those who have lively scientific and biological interests every detail becomes fascinating. If this were a book for married people I would not hesitate to plunge into a lengthy description, but I am here concerned rather with the attitudes and behaviour that precede marriage. Those who want detailed knowledge should not be afraid to seek it, and if the reader is, say, a sixth-form biologist, and can bear the elaboration of technical terminology that is to be found in embryology, he should ask a medical friend to lend him *Human Embryology* by Hamilton, Boyd, and Mossman. This book, beautifully printed and illustrated, contains far more than any lay reader can understand, but there are parts here and there worth following carefully, for to understand the development of a few of the organs is to recognize the complexity, beauty, and mystery of the most astonishing process in the whole of nature.

We live in an age in which complex man-made machines are held in great respect; automobiles, aeroplanes, atomic reactors, and electronic computers are almost the gods of our time. We think of them as though they were greater than the people who designed and made them. Yet the humblest baby, growing in nine months from a microscopic blob of jelly to a perfect living body, has a complexity and a beauty of coordination that puts the most elaborate computer to shame. Because human beings and babies are so common, the mystery and wonder of their bodies are taken for granted, and most people are content to know less about them than they know about the gear-boxes of their cars.

Many boys – perhaps most – are allowed to get the feeling that the knowledge of pregnancy and birth is 'for women only', that the details are rightly a matter for hushed conversation between mothers and that it is wrong for a boy to want to know about them. Unfortunately there often goes with this a feeling that there is something inharmonious and incompatible between the idealistic adoration that he feels for the beautiful body of his girl friend and the distortion of a woman's body that takes place when she is with child.

This is as deplorable as it is widespread. It is important that you should realize that you are entitled to all the knowledge you want; nothing need be thought of as taboo. Some of the information is even finding its way into biology textbooks for schools. Forty years ago biology textbooks were few and they tended to stop at the reproductive system of the frog.

The next step was to discuss the reproduction of the rabbit, and eventually a very good textbook was published which dared to mention fertilization and pregnancy in women. Later, with the encouragement of such organizations as the Social Biology Council and the British Medical Association, several clearly written books or pamphlets were available and more people now marry with the knowledge they ought to have. Many young married couples find a great joy in pregnancy, and to a man who is free from guilt about physical interests, the changes in his wife's body and the evidences of the living creature growing within are a source of interest and pleasure, and often amusement. So don't be afraid of knowledge; you may find some day that knowledge and tenderness go together.

To show how attitudes are changing I think I should mention that husbands are now sometimes encouraged to be present at the birth of a child, possibly even to make themselves useful, instead of being shut out and getting worked up with unhelpful anxiety. But the most delightful story on this theme that I have heard came from an older generation, from a man who at the time of telling it was a humble member of Britain's two million unemployed. He had once been a pioneer farmer in Canada and, with no obstetric knowledge whatever, had to deliver his wife of twins, for there was no midwife or doctor within fifty miles and the birth was early. He told me with joy and pride how, after the birth, he held one on each hand – 'no bigger than chickens, about three pounds each'. Both lived and, when I knew this man, they were two good-looking girls in their teens.

If you start off, as some boys and young men do, with a feeling of revulsion when the biological aspect of a girl's body is brought to your notice, when menstruation, pregnancy, or birth are mentioned, then I think you should try to get this straight before you are married. You might be helped to overcome the feeling by including young married couples among your friends, people of the sort who really enjoy all their experiences together and who are sometimes prepared to talk frankly about them.

There are certain facts about pregnancy which everyone should know, whether they contemplate marriage eventually or not, and for this reason I want to give at least a brief description of what happens from conception to birth. Assuming that intercourse has occurred at a favourable time during the month, there will be sperm cells swimming up the Fallopian tubes and nearing the fringed ends just when a follicle bursts and an ovum is swept into one of the tubes. A number of sperms may attach themselves to the ovum, but only one is allowed to penetrate, and the others drop off. This one loses its tail when it enters the ovum and its head swells up until it resembles the nucleus of the ovum. It then joins with it, and the ovum, now said to be fertilized, has an enlarged nucleus with equal quantities of what one might call 'inheritance material' from both parents. The ova that a woman produces month by month are not all alike; they differ from one another in the selection of her characteristics that they carry in the chromosomes – the tiny thread-like structures contained by the nucleus. Similarly the sperm cells differ from one another as to what particular balance of the man's characteristics they carry. So what the baby inherits depends upon which egg cell is fertilized by which sperm cell. At the moment the union takes place, the matter is settled. From that point on the mother's body is simply a place of nourishment and protection and nothing that she does or thinks will alter the sex of the baby or its characteristics. The baby could be injured by a disease passed on to it by the mother, but fortunately a baby in the womb is remarkably resistant to disease and germs cannot easily pass across the placenta which joins the pregnant mother to her child.

As the fertilized ovum moves down the Fallopian tube towards the uterus it divides into two cells. The nucleus first divides, making two nuclei, each exactly like the one nucleus from which they were made. Then the blob of protoplasm separates into two blobs, with one nucleus in each. It is not known how long it takes for one division of this sort to take place, but suppose that it takes twelve hours and that each of the two new cells divided in two after another twelve hours. At the end of the day there will be four cells; after a day and a half, eight; and two days, sixteen. At each division the number will be doubled and after ten days there will be over a million cells in the group. It may take about this time for the ovum to move down the tube and become attached to the surface of the womb. You can imagine it looking after two or three days like a microscopic raspberry and then, as the days go on, becoming much more complicated. Compared with most cells, an ovum before it begins to divide is very large but when it has reached the complicated stage its cells are much smaller. When the structure is ready to be embedded in the womb it has about ten times the diameter of the original ovum, and the cells on its surface have developed the peculiar property of being able to burrow into the tissue on the inside surface of the womb. So the cluster sinks in, making a pit for itself and becoming surrounded by a little pool of the mother's blood. This pit is sealed on the outside by a clot.

The cluster, still called an ovum though it consists of a great number of cells, sends out little shoots, called *villi*, into the tissue of the womb. These serve to anchor the ovum and, later, blood vessels develop inside these villi connected with the body of the embryo. Oxygen and food-chemicals diffuse from the mother's blood through the villi into the baby's blood; the two bloods do not actually come into contact with each other.

Inside the ovum a small group of cells begins to bend and fold until it looks a bit like a body, with a head and a tail and a bulge where the heart is going to be. After two months from the very beginning this embryo has become unmistakably the body of a child, though the head is large and out of proportion. The whole body is at this stage only about an inch long, but limb-buds have grown out into definite limbs with fingers and toes. Indeed every organ is present in the body at least in rudimentary form, and for the remaining seven months of pregnancy (or *gestation*) the structure has only to increase in size and change in its proportions. From this time on it is no longer called an embryo, but a foetus.

The womb is now increasing in size and there is a bulge on its inside surface, where the foetus is growing, surrounded by its membranes. It is like a hollow ball with the foetus hanging inside, and where the ball is fixed to the surface of the uterus there is a mass of villi now called the *placenta*. The blood from the foetus travels out of its body, through the 'stalk' by which it hangs, into the villi of the placenta where it becomes enriched from the mother's blood, and then back into its body. You could not easily tell at this stage whether the foetus is male or female, for both look female to begin with, having between the legs what looks like the cleft of a girl's sexual parts, with the inner and outer lips. Where the lips join in front there is a swelling. In the case of a male foetus this enlarges and becomes the tip of the penis. The two inner lips grow together all along,

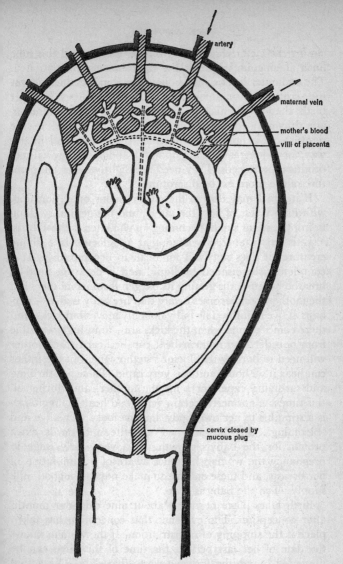

Fig. 5. Uterus and Foetus

Showing how the latter is nourished from the mother's blood through the walls of the villi. The placenta is shown in diagrammatic and simplified form. The foetus is about one inch long at the beginning of the third month.

closing the cleft, which then becomes a tube, and this tube finds an opening through the tip I have just mentioned. The two outer lips become hollow and join together to form the scrotum. At a much later stage, sometimes even after birth, the testes, which are first formed up in the abdomen, are drawn down until they are properly seated in the scrotum. It is important that they should descend in this way, for so long as they are up in the abdomen they will not produce sperm cells. They need the slightly lower temperature of the more exposed scrotum.

If it is a female foetus the cleft remains open, forming, with its two sets of lips, the vulva, and the genital swelling in front remains small, becoming known later as the clitoris.

It is important to realize that the foetus is a living creature; it does not wait for birth to become alive. It is completely surrounded by liquid and it does not need to breathe because it is getting its oxygen from its mother. But the mother soon becomes aware that her baby is alive – perhaps at five months. The baby not only moves but kicks, and there comes a time when the kicks are – amusingly – visible from outside. Also its heartbeat can be heard (the mother will need to borrow the doctor's stethoscope, but the father can hear it without) and it is very rapid. These are thrilling and satisfying experiences for the mother, and during all this time she normally feels in very good health. Pregnancy is a stimulus to her own body and she looks very alive and 'blooming'. She has a good appetite and needs extra protein for the baby's growth. At a very early stage in pregnancy the woman becomes aware of a stimulation of her breasts, and these enlarge to make possible a good milk supply when the baby is born.

Birth takes place normally about nine calendar months after conception. The evidence that conception has taken place is the stopping of menstruation. If the woman knows the date of her last period, the time of the birth can be predicted by adding forty weeks to that date. The actual fertilization takes place about half-way between periods, so that makes thirty-eight weeks from conception to birth.

Birth is a much safer experience than it used to be. It is now common practice for a woman to be seen frequently by her doctor throughout pregnancy so that any difficulties are known well in advance and surgical assistance is ready if it is required. The greatest danger in childbirth used to be from puerperal fever – a streptococcal infection that was carried from one woman to another through midwives and doctors who did not wash their hands and used no antiseptic. Every intelligent person ought to know something of the history of medicine and there is no more dramatic story in it than that of the discovery by Semmelweiss, working in a Vienna maternity hospital, of the way in which puerperal fever was transmitted, and of his tragic fight against his jealous and unhygienic superiors.*

But though childbirth has become an experience to which a mother longing for a child can look forward happily and without fear, there are still some women who die of infection or haemorrhage – usually those who try to get rid of an unwanted baby by abortion. To explain this I must first distinguish the ways in which a pregnancy may come to an end before its proper time.

Miscarriage and Abortion

Miscarriage is the term usually applied to an accidental premature birth, taking place some time during the first seven months and therefore nearly always involving the death of the foetus. This is apt to happen with some women more than others and they have to be specially careful, when they 'try again', to live quietly during pregnancy. It is disappointing and upsetting but need never be a reason for despair.

The term abortion is sometimes used in the same sense, but more often it means an early expulsion deliberately induced, with intent to get rid of the foetus. It is sometimes carried out by a doctor if the mother's physical or mental

---

* The story is well told in *Devils, Drugs, and Doctors* by William Haggard, published by Heinemann.

health would be endangered by a continued pregnancy and normal birth. This is legal, but the signed agreement of a second doctor is necessary.

An abortion carried out in any other circumstances is a criminal abortion. A doctor carrying it out, for instance, to oblige a patient who wants to avoid having an illegitimate baby, is guilty of a punishable crime. There are 'quacks', unregistered medical men or 'chemists', and women who make a business of it, to whom girls sometimes go. Even if a girl attempts to 'procure an abortion' by interfering with her own body it is a crime in the eyes of the law. Quite apart from the criminal aspect, abortions carried out by drugs or surgery, in any circumstances other than those legalized, are exceedingly dangerous. The womb is one of the most easily infected organs, and only the most scrupulous medical care, with all the facilities of a hospital at hand, can make certain that abortion is safe – safe from haemorrhage, septicaemia, and death. No one should ever listen to anyone who says he or she knows somebody who will do it. A man who encourages or helps his girl to have an abortion is an 'accessory before the fact' and can be punished. Illegal abortion is now thought by some to be as serious a social problem as venereal disease.*

An *induction*, by the way, is a perfectly legitimate medical practice. It is a hastening of the normal birth some time during the last week or two if the foetus is already rather large, or after full-term if the baby is 'late'.

Birth

At full-term, about nine months after conception, the foetus weighs on an average between seven and eight pounds. It lies in the uterus head downwards with the

*The Abortion Act of 1968 has given a much greater freedom of discretion to doctors in deciding whether an abortion is justifiable. But the degree to which this freedom is used varies greatly from place to place, according to the outlook of the surgeons and the facilities available for the operation. The situation at present – 1969 – is therefore somewhat confused.

20-inch umbilical cord round its body. This umbilical cord carries the two hypogastric arteries and the umbilical vein which take the blood to and from the placenta to be refreshed by being brought near to the mother's blood in the villi. Occasionally live babies are born as early as seven months, but they are then small and have to be carefully looked after if they are to survive.

The baby lies completely surrounded by a watery liquid – the *amniotic fluid* – held in the double-walled bag made out of the original wall of the ovum (*chorion*) and the amniotic sac (*amnion*) in which the embryonic plate first developed. It is not known for certain what 'triggers off' the process of birth, but the woman begins to experience muscular contractions, recurring at fairly long intervals. Later these become more rapid. The large developed uterus is a very muscular organ and what the mother feels is the contraction of the muscle fibres. The inner end of the uterus begins to contract and thus ease the foetus downwards, while longitudinal muscle strands begin to pull the cervix – the mouth of the womb – back over the head. A 'bag of waters' is trapped, usually beyond the head of the child, and there comes a stage at which this bursts. It helps to expand the passages gently, and the water surrounding the baby eases the birth.

In the most usual position, the head is born first and opens the way for the rest of the body to slip out easily. The head of the baby passes through the opening of the pelvis in a diagonal position usually with the brow towards the back of the mother's body. The bones of the head are soft and can overlap a little when moving through the passages. When the head emerges, the rest of the body, being smaller and very plastic (the bones are like rubber, not yet calcified), slips out easily. This final stage can be very quick.

The contractions of the uterus are automatic, but in the later stages of labour the woman can cooperate deliberately, using the abdominal muscles to help in the process of birth. When the baby is born it is still connected by the umbilical cord with the placenta inside the mother's body.

45

Although the placenta – which develops from the outside of the ovum – is a large mass of tissue about eight inches in diameter embedded in the wall of the uterus, there is a neat provision for its detachment. There is a layer of cells, called somewhat humorously the postage-stamp-layer, which, like the perforated edge of a stamp, will tear away easily. By further contractions of the uterus the whole placenta comes away and is pushed out of the body. It is normal practice to tie the umbilical cord in two places near the baby's abdomen and cut between the ties. The stump eventually withers leaving the familiar 'belly-button'.

There is nearly always some bleeding from the uterus, but the rapid shrinking after the placenta has been expelled squeezes up the blood vessels and prevents the bleeding from being too great. During the next few weeks the uterus continues to shrink in size, its mass of tissues being 're-digested' into the body until it regains its former size (no bigger than a small pear).

When the baby is born it must first be encouraged to breathe. It must cry, because this act opens its lungs and starts up the circulation of the blood through them. Otherwise it would quickly die, being deprived of the oxygen previously obtained through the umbilical vein from its mother. If it doesn't cry it must be carefully made to do so ! The baby is washed to remove the greasy lubricating material with which it is naturally covered and its eyes carefully cleaned and sterilized from any possibility of gonococcal infection. It can be put to the breast fairly soon. It doesn't get much to drink at first, for the mother's milk supply is not in full flow until about four days from the birth. But the experience of the breast and the comfort of the mother's body is an immediate necessity to this little creature suddenly shot out from the complete comfort and security of the womb into a cold world.

If the mother is just a girl, say nineteen, the whole process, from the first contractions to the final stage of birth, can be very quick and the baby may be there before the husband has had time to get the doctor. Older women are usually in

labour with their first child a little longer. Men are sometimes dreadfully worried about the pains that women
experience in childbirth – more than their wives are themselves. Much depends upon a woman's attitude, for fear and
anxiety tend to tighten up the body when it should be
relaxed; a husband who is steady and reassuring is therefore a considerable help and a panicky one a nuisance.
Some doctors believe that birth can be almost painless given
the right physical condition and mental attitude. This may
be true, but when some of these doctors assert that birth is
often painless among native peoples they are vigorously
contradicted by explorers who have been present at births.

To get your feelings right about all this, you must recognize that pain is not the worst thing that any of us have to
face. Indeed we are built to take it, and women just as
much as men. Painful experiences are no more and no less
to be deplored in women than in men. A woman who has a
loving and trustworthy husband can bear almost anything
and the discomfort of childbirth is quickly forgotten in the
joy of being a mother. The maternity ward in a hospital is
one of the happiest of places.

4

SEXUAL INTERCOURSE

IT is a pity that we haven't a simple single word that we can happily accept instead of the roundabout phrases and Latin words that we use for this activity. *Sexual intercourse*, *copulation*, *coition* are clumsy or ugly, *mating* is more applicable to animals, *making love* might apply to any expression of feeling, trivial or deep, and the only single word of English origin has come to express a violence that should have no place in love. 'Going to bed with . . .' is a phrase often used, but it gives the slightly stuffy impression that the only right place for love-making is in bed. There are yet looser phrases such as 'having an affair with . . .' which may imply complete intimacy or may not.

A great deal of talk goes on between boys about sexual intercourse. Their thoughts about sex usually become closely focused on the sex act itself; they think about it, they wonder about it, they make jokes about it. Long before they have actually experienced it, many boys will enjoy being suspected of having 'done it' to a girl. A boy really believed to have done it acquires a great prestige. It is a fact that a certain number of boys do experience intercourse while they are still at school, perhaps through having found the sort of girl who is not properly looked after at home and is therefore loose and uncontrolled in her conduct. But very many boys, though they talk about it, and even brag about their 'experience', in fact know little about sexual intercourse.

All this makes it necessary to say something definite about the sex act, so that there may be no doubt about what it is like in certain essential respects. It *can* be very similar to what takes place between animals. It is a fact that boys often get their first impressions of intercourse from watching animals mating, and they take it that human mating is similar. Thus it seems that it is an action done to the female by the male, an action that is urgent, hasty, and crude. There are indeed human beings who carry it out in this way. The woman, though she may invite love-making by preliminary love-play and flirtation, in the act becomes completely submissive, experiences little tenderness, and is perhaps physically hurt. The man gets a brutal satisfaction by dominating the woman. He 'triumphs' over her.

Love-making that is fully human is not at all like this; it is an equal-sided experience. Though the woman may appear outwardly to play a submissive part, she is not passively submissive, but actively and eagerly so. She may even be as physically active as her partner, both in commencing the act and maintaining it. In times past it was commonly held that a woman who eagerly and unashamedly enjoyed the sex act was not a nice woman; she was a hussy, a bad lot. This was an appalling injustice to women; it took away much of the joy of marriage and did a great deal of mental harm. The idea isn't exactly dead, but you will not find a single modern book written by a doctor or a psychologist in support of it. It is now generally thought that the act should not only be a delight to both man and woman throughout, but that it should end, for the woman as well as for the man, in the climax of an orgasm. For the man this occurs in the vigorous nervous spasm that drives the seminal fluid out of the penis, for the woman in a more diffuse but equally satisfying discharge of nervous tension, leading to complete relaxation.

At its best, between sensitive people with deep feelings, it is not usually something that just happens suddenly. It is led up to by a series of thoughts, feelings, and actions heightening their awareness of how much they enjoy each other and mean to each other. The beginning of this may be in something that apparently has nothing to do with sex, something that they have enjoyed together and that has made them feel keenly alive. Tenderness is the outstanding characteristic of intercourse between such people. This does not mean that it is not a vigorous experience. The man may be physically very much the active aggressive male and the woman will enjoy him in this part. But there will be a sort of amusement that springs out of their tenderness for each other and that prevents the 'aggression' from being coarse and primitive. The man will enjoy 'doing it' and the woman enjoy having it 'done to her' and each know quite well that they are equally eager and active. This is an example of what I have said previously, that in human activity at its best we do not leave behind any part of our nature; we take it all with us, but we change its quality by deepening its relationship to the whole.

The woman is often hurt to some extent by the first attempts at intercourse. Some women have a thick hymen covering most of the opening of the vagina, and to have this penetrated causes a sudden, sharp pain which may be quite acute. Bleeding usually happens. In view of this, the greatest gentleness is called for in the man; he must be prepared to make several cautious attempts before complete intercourse can properly occur; and these may be spread over several days or even a week or two. In some instances the physical hurt may prevent any enjoyment until stretching and healing are complete. Other women have a negligible hymen and intercourse may be completed at the first attempt.* But there will always be some hurt to the woman. If it is not too great it will not stand in the way of enjoyment. A woman may even take a pleasure in being slightly hurt by a man whom she wholly trusts and loves. Any hurt will, however, be very disturbing if the woman has reason to feel that the man is uncertain of his love for her or is treating her casually. This, and the bitter sense of lost self-respect, produces much of the distress felt by girls as a result of irresponsible sexual experience indulged in 'for fun'.

Even a woman used to intercourse will suffer pain from a hasty attempt on the part of the man. She has to be fully roused, as stimulated and urgent as he is, before her vagina

* The apparent absence of a hymen is not necessarily proof that a woman has had previous sexual experience.

is in a condition to receive his penis. The chief evidence of her readiness is in the activity of Bartholin's glands, producing the lubricating fluid that moistens the vulva and vagina. This implies that the act must be preceded by a great deal of what is called love-play, which involves intimate caressing and perhaps the exchange of many thoughts, both grave and gay.

In view of the fact that this book may be read by young men about to enter upon sex experience, and that it may perhaps be the only book read by them, I should say that there *is* a certain physical inequality between men and women that is sometimes difficult to overcome. In a normal man the orgasm easily and inevitably happens, the experience comes to an end, and he often wants to go to sleep. In a woman the most sensitive organ, the clitoris, is some distance from the vagina and may not receive any stimulation unless there is a deliberate intention that it should. We might expect nature to have made the vagina alone sufficiently stimulable to make an orgasm certain, but the fact is that in many women it is not so. Many women do not have any orgasm during the first year of marriage, and many never have it at all while the penis is in the vagina. They get it only through the man's being sufficiently thoughtful to caress the clitoris during the act or afterwards.

The effect of civilization may be responsible for difficulties of this sort. This is not intended to be a handbook to marriage, but I feel the need to put in here a practical point. I believe that overmuch reading, talking, and thinking about sexual behaviour creates some of the very difficulties they are intended to avert. A great deal has been written in recent years about the necessity for female orgasm; the result is that women become increasingly anxious about it, and this very anxiety prevents it from happening. It is far better not to worry about it and be prepared to wait. The how-to-do-it books have made success on the physical side of sex too immediately important. Among people who are very happily married there is a wide variety of experience in this matter of 'physical adjustment'. Some achieve it quickly, some slowly. The physical is *not* the most important side, certainly not the side to be concerned about first. If there is a deep personal relationship, difficulties about the physical side will often come right without too much attention to 'technique'.

When I talk to boys about the sex act I have to answer numerous detailed questions. *How long does it take?* The answer is anything from a few minutes to, say, half an hour. In the course of years people can develop a power of control that will delay the orgasm for a long time, and this enables them to enjoy a prolonged intimacy in which there may be long periods of stillness. *How often does it happen?* There are great variations in this. People who do not use any birth-control arrangements may not wish to have too many babies and may have infrequent intercourse. Between normally vigorous people who are eager to have a baby, or who use birth-control, it may be several times a week when they are first married. In middle life, especially when people are carrying heavy responsibilities in the outside world, it may be once a week or less. These are only rough averages. *Are there several positions in which the act can take place?* Yes. The commonest is one in which the woman lies on her back with her legs apart and the man lies between her legs and over her body, resting his weight on his elbows. But the positions can be reversed and the woman can lie or kneel astride the man. They can also lie on their sides facing each other. There are yet other positions; but the animal position, with the male on the back of the female, is rarely used by men and women. Their love for each other makes them want to face each other. It is entirely normal and wholesome for people who love each other to experiment with every possible variation; indeed it would be just plain dull to allow habit to take charge so that it was always done the same way in the same position. It need not always take place at night nor always in bed. It can take place, with great exhilaration, in lonely places out of doors. It is possible for people to say to each other after years of married life that it still happens to them as though it had never happened before; its freshness seems always to be renewed.

Is it a fact that women want it more at certain times of their month than at others? Yes, there is a tendency for them to be more easily roused to sexual desire at certain times, and this is often the time when intercourse is more likely to lead to the conception of a baby. But in the course of years women become rather less dominated by their menstrual cycle, and may be eager at almost any time. A man, however, should never assume that a woman ought to be ready to respond whenever he wants her. There are times when she does not want to be aroused, and at such times she should not be pressed. It does not mean that she doesn't love him at such times. *Does a woman cease to want intercourse after the menopause, the time round about 45 when she ceases to have periods?* Not necessarily. Indeed desire is likely to cease only if the woman expects it to; there is no real reason for it, and sexual enjoyment is possible for both men and women right into old age.

Does the sex act necessarily lead to the birth of a baby? No. Sometimes a baby begins to develop after the first love-making; sometimes a married couple has to wait years, in spite of frequent intercourse. A baby may never be conceived, and this will be on account of sterility in either the man or the woman. The man's seminal fluid may contain no sperms. The woman may be sterile because there is an obstruction in the Fallopian tube, preventing the ovum from moving down it to the uterus. (Medical skill, which should always be called upon in cases of sterility, can frequently put right whatever it is that is preventing a couple from having children.) In normal people there are many different factors that will affect the readiness or otherwise with which a baby comes, and it is impossible to predict. *How does a man feel about the baby part of it?* This is a more thoughtful question usually put to me by girls. A normal girl who has not been wrongly stirred up physically, or has not been involved in too much excitement in a trivial-minded group, will closely relate the act of making love with the possibility – a delightful one to her – of having a baby. Do men think this way? I wish I could say yes. Many undoubtedly do, and part of the excitement and pleasure of the sex act arises from the thought of giving the beloved what she most desires. But there is so much in our civilization that tears sex away from the family pattern and the responsibilities that it should normally carry. This specially encourages men to think of the sex act as an isolated act of pleasure which, helped by birth-control, can be cut off from any consequences. Though I have said 'in our civilization' I have to recognize that it has always been possible for men to be irresponsible; they do not have to bear the babies and they can quietly disappear.

Quite apart from this there *is* a difference between men and women, and it often seems a profound one. In a sense, sex is a woman's whole life. Often in marriage a woman's whole life is adjusted to her husband, his needs, and the thought of a family. Seen in this pattern, the sex act is not for her something that has a definite beginning and an end; it is continuous with her whole activity; it links up with everything she does in the home; the pleasure she takes in it is one with the activities of the rest of her day. But for the man it can be, and usually is, an incident. The impulse takes him and is gratified; he can quickly switch his thought from it to something else within a few minutes. Sexual activity is something he can fit in between having his supper and going to sleep, between tinkering with the car and arguing about politics. In spite of the obsessive way men often seem to talk about sex, it plays a far smaller part in their lives than it does in the lives of women.

But this is a generalization which will not be true in some individual cases. Moreover, there are wholesome influences at work even in our modern civilization which tend to increase men's enjoyment of family life. It is not difficult to find in many levels of present-day society an increasing tendency for men to share all the tasks of family life and the enjoyment of a baby's first years – things that nearly all men used to regard as outside their province. One of the most moving – and reassuring – sights at stations during wartime was the tenderness with which soldiers said good-bye to their babies.

How is birth-control (contraception) carried out? The man may cover his penis with a very thin latex sheath (condom) and this is intended to catch the seminal fluid. It is a bothersome, unpleasing way, because the partners cannot forget its presence. It might be thought a very certain way, but it is not. Pregnancies have resulted from the sheath slipping off inside the vagina, or from there being an imperfection in the condom itself. Other methods are used by the woman; the appliances can be fitted well in advance, and their presence is not felt during intercourse. One is a small rubber cap (an occlusive pessary), which fits tightly over the projecting cervix at the inner end of the vagina. Another is a much larger membrane with a stiff circular rim (Dutch cap) which springs out against the wall of the vagina so as to shut off the whole of the inner end. Both these caps are used with a contraceptive jelly or cream containing a chemical to make the sperms inactive. No contraceptive method is absolutely safe, and the methods used by the woman are certainly unsafe if the appliances are not of the right size. Clinics and doctors can be consulted to determine the size.

Is it true that there are 'safe periods'? A woman is most likely to conceive as a result of intercourse midway between menstrual periods, because that is about the time when the ovum leaves the ovary and begins to travel down the Fallopian tube. She is least likely to conceive as a result of intercourse just before or just after menstruating. Largely as a result of the controversy within the Roman Catholic Church and the Papal Encyclical, great attention has been given in the late nineteen-sixties to this method of reducing the number of pregnancies. It has been called the rhythm method. As ordinarily practised it is very unreliable. The woman may have irregular periods, upsetting calculations, and even second ovulations have been known. Spermatozoa may live for longer in the woman's body than we know.

I do not want to encourage anyone to use this method unless prepared to do so with intelligence and a full knowledge of the principles.* It is made *fully* reliable only by clearly detecting the point of ovulation: the woman takes her temperature each morning, for it rises by about a degree at ovulation and remains at this level until menstruation begins. A series of charts has to be made and carefully interpreted. It is clear that this is a method only for the intelligent and responsible.

The contraceptive Pill, by using hormones like those already in the body, alters the chemical cycle of events and suppresses ovulation. It is taken for three weeks of the month, thus allowing menstruation to take place normally. The danger that it increases in some women the possibility of thrombosis, the formation of a blood clot that interferes with circulation, is statistically much less than the danger, slight as it is, of dying in childbirth. In some women it causes depression or increase in weight. Again, it is a method that requires responsibility and care, an ability to establish a routine.

Lastly there is the coil, or intra-uterine device, a plastic loop inserted into the cavity of the uterus and left there permanently. It prevents the fertilised ovum from embedding itself. Its failure rate is two per cent; that is, two out of a hundred women using it become pregnant *per year*.

Many people, married or unmarried, practise *coitus interruptus*, withdrawing the penis just before orgasm, so that the seminal fluid is not discharged inside the vagina. It is not a good practice. I have no personal evidence from anyone, but its effects on both man and woman is said to be more disturbing than they realize; it may do harm to their feelings about intercourse. It is not even safe, for the moment is difficult to choose and seminal fluid may ooze out of the penis before the proper orgasm takes place.

*See *The Scientific Basis of the Infertile Period* by Dr John Marshall (Catholic Advisory Council).

5

THINKING ABOUT SEX, I

ANY teacher who keeps his ears open will be aware of the
ripe language in which a group of thirteen- or fourteen-
year-old boys indulges – especially if they are unaware of the
presence of an adult. It comes and goes in waves; sometimes
a group is fairly free from 'dirty language' while at other
times it becomes almost an obsession. It is an indiscriminate
mixture of lavatory words and sexual words and it makes
one wish sometimes that nature hadn't put our excretory
and sexual organs so close together at the tail end of our
bodies. I must add that it isn't only boys in the early teens
that indulge in this language. Girls can be caught up in it
and it can be as strong among them as among young men.
I found it among undergraduates when as a boy I went to a
certain university to take scholarship examinations and
had to sit with these undergraduates at table for a few
days. I was a sixth-former at a London grammar school;
but I had thought of undergraduates as men. I was stag-
gered to find some of them way back at the stage of early
childhood. They seemed not to have got beyond the interests evoked by all the fuss and bother of putting babies on
the pot. And for them, too, sex and excretion seemed to be
mixed up.

When I break in upon a group of boys using this sort of
language I sometimes say to them: 'You know what most
of these words mean. They are sexual words. Now what do
you think sex is *for*?' I usually get the bald reply – after a
little hesitation – that it's for producing babies.* When I
ask: 'But what are *you* using it for?' they only scratch their
heads and grin. Sometimes we sit down and talk about it

*They may be giving simply the answer they think is expected of
them. As discussion becomes more fearless, with the increased publicity
given to sexual matters, young boys and girls more readily acknowledge
the element of enjoyment in sexual contacts.

and then I am bombarded with a host of detailed questions. These show that there is a tremendous interest in sex, almost an obsession, long before boys are sufficiently mature to put the facts into any pattern of thought that can give them a feeling of goodness and satisfaction. I always get the same answer in reply to my question – the answer that sex is for producing babies. It is a perfectly rational – or biological – answer. But it does not occur to them that they are *using* sex for another purpose, and I cannot expect them to understand the great significance and use of sex quite apart from its use in producing more boys and girls.

Sex can be used in a great variety of ways, some desirable, others not. In times past children were often given the impression that the only good use of sex was for producing babies and that all other uses were bad. This was a most unfortunate impression because it made young people feel that all the desires and interests connected with sex that came flooding into their minds, and that had nothing immediately to do with babies, were wicked and guilty. Well-intentioned people, feeling that something had to be done to correct this wrong impression, began to say: 'There's nothing wrong with sexual desires and thoughts; they are quite natural. Sex is *good*.' As a result of this new idea other people began to say: 'Yes, sex is good; let's have lots of it!' Now look at the statement made by the well-intentioned people. It contains three assertions: that there is nothing wrong with sexual desires, that sexual desires are natural, that sex is good. Only one of these assertions is necessarily true: the one that says that sexual desires are natural. The other two assertions may be true or untrue according to the circumstances. It would be better to say that sex is neither good nor bad; it is the use we make of it that is good or bad. When revised in this way the statement obviously gives no excuse for having 'lots of sex'.

Other things can be thought of in this way. When there was no printing, books were laboriously copied by hand. Surely, then, printing when it came was a 'good thing'? But was it? Of course, you will say, it enables us to read the Bible,

Shakespeare, and the *Guardian*. You may even instance this book, if you like it, and show that because of the invention of printing I am able to reach thousands of young people instead of only the hundreds whom I meet as a teacher. To this I shall retort that for every word that is read in the Bible, thousands are read out of sensational rubbish, that Shakespeare cannot possibly compete in popularity with the comic strip, and that the circulation of the *Guardian* is very small compared with that of certain papers I must not name but which contain very unreliable political information among a mass of scandal, highly-coloured romance, pin-ups, and salacious reporting. Isn't it obvious that printing is neither good nor bad – but that it is the *use* of it that is good or bad? The same can be said about science; it is the *use* of it that has to be judged good or bad, according to whether the result is Calder Hall and penicillin or H-bombs and mustard gas.

It would be true to say that the invention of printing brought a new and very great *freedom*. This was the freedom to circulate the most valuable of men's thoughts and discoveries throughout the civilized world, so that men could communicate with each other across space and time, passing on all that was helpful and stimulating to millions of people who could never meet. But it also gave freedom to circulate the most poisonous thoughts, to stupefy millions with propaganda, to stop people thinking for themselves, to degrade their spiritual life and dirty their minds, and to put them into the power of a few unscrupulous men.

Sex too gives us tremendous freedom. Imagine what life would be like if the human race reproduced as an amoeba or a bacterium does, simply by the parent organism splitting in two, so that each of the young were exactly alike and just like the parent. Wouldn't life be dull, wouldn't we be confined to a miserably limited experience! The fact that we are sexual beings makes possible an intensely rich and interesting life; that is what I mean by freedom – the possibility of richness, variety, adventure, discovery. But the greater the freedom the greater is the possibility of its abuse. The abuse of printing and the abuse of atomic science are examples of this. It is equally evident in sexual life; nothing can take a man or woman deeper into depravity, suffering, and misery than the abuse of the possibilities that sex offers them.

At this moment I am not in the least concerned with conventions or morals. I know very well that under an appearance of the greatest respectability and conventionality just as much cruel abuse of sexual opportunity can go on as in a brothel. It isn't, on the other hand, that I have 'no use for conventions'; it is simply that I am trying to think in quite different terms so as to throw some light on problems that have been obscured by heated argument both from those who support convention and those who would smash it. Both the deliberately conventional person and the deliberately unconventional person are in fact slaves to convention, the one because he loves it, the other because he hates it; neither can get away from it. This has to be recognized before there can be any clear thinking about sex.

Now back to this subject of freedom. To say that sex gives us a form of freedom is also to say that we are at liberty to make a *choice* about it. If we automatically made good use of our freedom and couldn't do anything else, then the word 'good' would become quite meaningless. This is an important point and a very simple one, yet one that is startling to most people, especially to those who are too much concerned with making other people 'good'. The word 'good' only means what it does so long as we have the opposite to contrast it with. Freedom makes sense only if it is really open to us to choose *either* good *or* bad. Another point follows: we are free people only if we really do make a choice and do not allow ourselves to be pushed along by life like logs down a river. But choosing, deciding on a definite direction, involves getting on top of the situation and of ourselves. Now the log has become a boat, provided with engines and steering equipment. Choosing a point to aim for and getting towards it involves not only knowing about the currents in the river – the outside world – but also understanding the nature of the boat, what its engines are capable of, how its steering works, what can go wrong in particular conditions. Here the analogy breaks down, for each of us is not only the captain of the boat but also the boat itself. This makes the problem begin to be difficult.

Had I been writing a hundred years ago the difficulty would not have been so obvious. Then each person was usually regarded as the captain of his own ship – the captain of his soul if you like. If he took a wrong direction – well, he was just a bad captain, ill-advised or badly trained or just plain wicked. If a person took to burglary it was because he was a bad man. You could try to make him a good man and thus get him to stop his thieving habits, but there was no scientific attempt to find out why the man was 'bad'. He just had covetous feelings and so he stole. It was assumed that the reason why people did things were simply the reasons present in their minds at the moment. In the last fifty years, however, our idea of the reasons why people behave as they do has tremendously changed.

We have had to recognize, for instance, that often people do some surprising thing without being in the least able to give you a reason for it. Sometimes these actions are shocking or violent, quite 'out of character', and the person is left horrified at what he has done. Haven't you sometimes done something of this sort, gone hot all over afterwards and then rushed round to the people concerned, to say to them 'Please, oh please, I didn't mean it. I'm not like that really – not in the least!' But if that is true, why did you do it? Since this book is about sex I might mention some sexual examples. Now and then you will read in the papers of some well-known and even highly respected person being brought to trial for a sexual offence that revolts you. He has behaved shockingly in a public lavatory or tried to do something sexual to a little child. Most of the people who know the man may be quite incredulous, and it may be true to say that he is in most respects a good man. An impulse took hold of him and he did something quite out of character. Further, he is as horrified afterwards as anyone else and he can't explain it.

In the Middle Ages we should have said that a devil entered into him for a few moments. Today we say that we do not know all of ourselves; we only know the surface of our own minds and there exist under the surface many impulses and reasons for action that we know nothing about. Since Freud, this has been known as the unconscious mind. It is recognized that many of the reasons why we do things are not to be found in the reasons we have in our conscious minds at the time, but are really in the unconscious. Many children steal and many of them steal sweets. The reason they give is the obvious one: 'because I wanted them, of course'. But it is found that a high proportion of these pilferers are children who have unsatisfactory homes, and parents who have not given them enough loving care. Even if they are given sweets by an understanding teacher so that there is no need to pilfer, they still do it. Obviously there is a reason they are not aware of. What we think is that it is not sweets they really want or need, but love. Sweets have become for them the symbols of love or the substitutes for it, but they do not know this. I can't multiply examples, but there is now a great mass of evidence to show that we rarely know the whole reason why we do things; there are deeper reasons that we do not recognize and these have their roots in the long-forgotten past.

Now it may be rather frightening to think you might experience some ungovernable impulse that could land you in serious trouble. Don't worry about that. Such instances are very rare indeed, just as murders are rare, but they are headlined by newspapers. No, what we have to worry about is the many subtle ways in which our everyday life can be directed by the unconscious and thus produce results that we don't intend. So very often, when friends, lovers, or husbands and wives quarrel and hurt each other, they haven't any clear idea why it has happened. They are bewildered by what has boiled up out of something seemingly quite trivial. Neither of them *intended* to hurt. Yet they *did* hurt and they *are* hurt and they can't easily get over it. The reason is that there is far more in both of them down below the level of their conscious thoughts and feelings than they ever suspected. They can get over their troubles only if they are both humble enough to admit the existence of this other part of themselves and really try to understand it. I think we can do much to understand what is happening 'down below' and thus become more genuinely in control of ourselves. Remember that what we are aiming at is to be really free, and we are not free if that stowaway below decks is in fact the chap who is doing the steering. We can't throw him overboard; we need him because he also does the stoking. But we can begin to understand him and get some cooperation.

I could not possibly deal in this book with the deeper problems of human behaviour, even if I felt competent to do so. But if I try to deal with some of the lighter problems it may help you to reflect on your conduct in a way which will lead to some understanding. If I come to any conclusions, I don't even want to claim them as correct; experts with more knowledge than I might come to different conclusions. I am just trying to point out a way of thinking that might begin to make sense of the otherwise puzzling behaviour of human beings, and might also show why the results of our actions are so often different from what we expect or intend. At several points later in this book I shall refer to the idea of unconscious impulses or reasons for our behaviour.

I began this chapter with a reference to dirty language. How often do boys ask themselves why they use it, and if they did ask themselves, what could they answer? Think of the words commonly used. The characteristic of them all seems to be the violence they express. But why should the boys want to be violent, and why should they choose sexual words to express violence? Here is a possible answer. Boys have a good deal of energy, and when it is uncontrolled it can be destructive. Valuable things can get broken and a home made difficult for the adults to live in. So the adults exert authority; they 'sit on' the boy. They make rules, they hedge him round with regulations, and make him suffer if he doesn't observe them. He can't rebel much in action because it gets him into trouble; so he rebels in his attitudes, and goes around letting off steam in his language. But why does he choose sexual words; why not be content with 'bloody' and 'damn'? Perhaps this is the reason. People have always been afraid of sex, because of its tremendous power – its power to destroy happiness, to set people against each other, to make a wreckage of life. They are afraid of the way sex comes surging up in the thoughts and impulses of the young. So they have tried to control it by pushing it under, insisting that it must not be talked about, that it must be 'taboo'. Now if you know that a certain word stands for something terribly important and at the same time is never to be spoken, then you get a tremendous feeling of letting off steam if you go away into a room by yourself and say that very word to the walls and the furniture. If an everyday thing like the potato had been regarded for hundreds of years as very powerful and at the same time unmentionable, then no doubt a boy would find great satisfaction in expressing his anger with another boy by calling him a potato.

There may be other reasons. I have observed that some boys are very given to sexual swearing if relations between father and mother have gone seriously wrong. Perhaps the unconscious part of their mind is saying something like this: 'Sex has smashed up my family and destroyed my home; all right then, I'll throw dirt at it.' But of course they don't *know* this. They just – swear.

Now supposing that this sort of explanation seems to make sense. Does it leave us still caught in the habit of sexual swearing? Or can we now begin to look at it from outside and do something to set ourselves free? It is a sad misuse of sex to use it for expressing anger, annoyance, vindictiveness, and repudiation when we know that it can be used for expressing the deepest tenderness for a beloved person, when it can be an expression of delight and content.

There's another fact that most of you will recognize; this sort of language is connected with a feeling of guilt. It is difficult to be sure where this feeling of guilt comes from. You do know that you tend to stop when a person you specially respect approaches, but you hardly know why. You just feel guilty about the impulse. It may be that we are bound to feel guilty because of the disapproval of society, because of the 'taboo' that I have mentioned. But it may be that there is some inherent sensitiveness in all of us – more in some than in others – that makes us aware when we are misusing something that might be made good. Whatever the explanation, the guilt is something to be troubled about, for it is difficult to get rid of it when the opportunity comes to make something good out of our sexual impulses. You will fall in love and feel an urge to make love to your girl, and then you will remember that the word most commonly used for the ultimate act of love is a repulsive word used to express the opposite of love. Will it be surprising if you wonder about the goodness of your desires?

What I have said about bad language applies also, perhaps more strongly, to 'dirty stories'. Bad language can be an unthinking habit, one that can pass away and be largely forgotten in a wholesome growing up. But the stories are often a much more deliberate attempt to make an evil use of sex, and therefore they leave a deeper sense of guilt. Now sex is often really funny, and I'm not suggesting that we should completely cease to be amused and to pass on our amusement. But the quite deliberate effort to push sex deeper into the mire in order to produce a yet more outrageous story has an effect on people that may remain with them for a long time. So it is worth while to stop and think why, and if some light is gained by this thinking then a release may be possible. It is good to try to obtain this release, to get some control and direction of our sexual interests, for we already have quite enough to contend with in what comes from outside. The world parades before our eyes every instance of sex-gone-wrong, assault, rape, seduction, multiple divorce, indecency, and incest. Sex achieving its proper object in good family life, permanent friendship, continued love, and a vigorous contribution to the community – that is all too normal to be worthy of a reporter's notice. We ought to ask whether all this reporting of sex-gone-wrong is affecting our thoughts and behaviour. By the way, don't blame the reporter. You are just as much to blame. Here are two things that could be reported in a paper:

Mr Blank returned home on Tuesday night very drunk. When his wife protested he attacked her with a chopper. She is in hospital suffering from multiple injuries. A neighbour called the police and Mr Blank was arrested after fierce resistance.

Mr Blank returned home on Tuesday night very tired after a tough day at the mill. Mrs Blank, who had also had a worrying day because of a sick child, had, however, taken the trouble to cook an unusually interesting meal. They both felt much the better for it and spent a restful evening watching T.V.

Which of these would you expect and want to see in the local paper? Ask yourself why. It may be an exercise in understanding your own unconscious mind.

6

THINKING ABOUT SEX, II

THE last chapter was intended to encourage you to begin to think about sex in such a way as to 'sort it all out' in relation to the rest of life. Now I want to consider – or ask you to consider – your own private thoughts. Only you know what these are, but I suspect that they are much the same as most other boys' private thoughts. Some people are more thoughtful than others. Some boys, especially those who are involved in gangs and spend most of their time talking and playing with others, don't do much thinking. They tend to accept what others think and do as others do. It would be well for them to stop and think sometimes; otherwise they have no freedom; they merely do as others do and have little individuality. But some boys do a great deal of 'inner thinking'; they turn their thoughts very much upon themselves and often get worried about themselves. Sex becomes disturbing to them and they can't just accept it as the gang accepts it. They perhaps feel a deep sense of guilt whenever they think about sex or after they have let a sexual impulse take charge of them. By the way, there are two ways of dealing with the guilt feeling. Often the boy in the gang is hardly conscious of it at all. If he feels it for a moment he can subdue it by rushing off into more gang activity, more excitement. He can ease it by telling himself that all the other chaps have the same interests and do the same things as he does. This doesn't mean that he gets rid of guilt. Some of the outrageous things that gangs do are evidence of the deep disturbance caused 'down below' because they won't face their guilt.

But all normal boys do *some* inner thinking. Many do a great deal, with much resulting unhappiness; they remain conscious of their guilt and try to cope with it. Some of the most sensitive and valuable personalities experience the greatest disturbance about sex. The inner thinking is very much confused, so if for the purposes of writing about it I sort it out a bit, it doesn't mean that it is as clearly marked off in fact. There is the thinking that arises from the development of the boy's own body. Before the arrival of puberty – the stage when the pubic hair begins to grow – a boy is interested in his body, but in a quick-come-and-go way. His mind may be on it for a moment and then on something else. The interest is not reflective. He may not take much notice of the fact that his penis sometimes becomes stiff and erect, or if he does, he may later completely forget it. Little boys masturbate – play with their penises – sometimes quite absent-mindedly in a mooning sort of way and at other times, especially in the presence of others, in a laughing superficial thoughtless way. But at puberty a boy begins to think about what he is doing; he not only has feelings and sensations, but he feels his feelings, so to speak; he is acutely conscious of the peculiar quality of them. He becomes more aware of himself as a distinct separate individual who is going through something, alone and away from others. This is a very normal and necessary part of growing up, and it is unfortunate if it is side-tracked by too much group activity, too much life in the mob. Being lonely, going through a phase of loneliness, is a necessary preparation for becoming a really understanding friend and member of your community in later life. It is in this loneliness that you begin to discover yourself.

You may be bound to feel that you are quite different from anyone else and that no other boy has to face quite what you have to face; but I think I can safely assure you that you are not being called upon to face more than you are fit to face. Some boys carry this feeling of difference too far and imagine that they are neurotic or unbalanced, when nothing of the kind is true.

Your private thoughts may seem to be full of obsessions, urgencies, longings that cannot be satisfied, fantasies, and dreams. Sometimes the obsessions – by which I mean intense continued thinking about something sexual from which you cannot detach yourself – arise from your having been denied knowledge that you really ought to have had. The majority of parents still fail to tell their children the facts about sex, or leave it till it is too late. They suffer from a curious embarrassment that stands in the way. Children ought to be told these things as soon as they ask about them, and if they are not afraid of their parents this will be at five or even sooner. They should then be told just as much as they can understand and no more. They will ask further questions in later years if they are given this good start. Failure to give children this knowledge, and especially the embarrassment that is behind this failure, makes the child feel that the knowledge is something dark and secret. Even after a boy knows the main facts he will still be obsessed with the details. He will perhaps go to the public library and consult the Encyclopaedia Britannica under the heading *Reproduction*. That must happen very often, for those pages in every library copy are the most worn and finger-marked! As the boy sits there reading he will be ready quickly to turn over the page to some other subject if someone seems about to pass behind him. And he feels hot and guilty about the interest. Poor boy – it's all so unnecessary! The situation should have eased a great deal since I was a boy. There are several popular books with the same sort of information as I have given in the earlier chapters. It has even found its way into some biology textbooks used in schools, and you can now answer questions on the subject in G.C.E.

Co-educational schools have been among the pioneers in getting this subject out into the open, and long before most other schools dared to do it they were including sexual anatomy in their classes. It was necessary that it should happen, and it proved good. If you have boys and girls together most of the time, and especially if it is a boarding-school, you would be asking for trouble if you didn't tell them all that they needed to know about each other's bodies. To be reminded all the time of the existence of the other sex by their presence, and to be denied knowledge about them, would be fantastic. Further, it has proved possible in such schools to talk about these matters with boys and girls together without a single snigger being heard, nor any embarrassment being felt by the teacher or his pupils. They take it soberly and seriously. You, the reader, may not be able to experience such conditions, but the knowledge of them may help you to feel that there is no occasion for you to feel guilty about what seem to you to be your obsessive interests.

All this has been concerned with getting straightforward biological information. But the boy who gets this information does not regard it just as he regards information about the stomach or the brain. He also has sexual feelings about it. He can read about the brain or stomach and then forget about them except in so far as he needs the knowledge for school purposes. But his sexual apparatus is unusually sensitive and he cannot help but be reminded of its existence several times a day. Moreover there are times when it seems almost to demand attention and there's no controlling it. This sets a problem and there is no simple solution. The problem arises principally because in civilized society marriage and sexual experience have to be postponed until many years after both boy and girl have become physically capable of sexual intercourse and parenthood. Some girls could have a baby at twelve, a boy could become a father perhaps at fourteen, but neither is capable of bearing the responsibilities of marriage or intercourse at so early an age. So they have to wait; and in the meantime their bodies become more and more urgent. Is this a bad thing? Not if it is wisely dealt with. Most of the great achievements of the human race have come out of a conflict, some sort of struggle within people or with conditions in the world outside them. They haven't come out of an arm-chair life, a life in which you get things just when you want them. The struggle that results through having to postpone sex experience until long after we first want it is part of the process that makes us into *persons*, the process I have already described in which we are conscious of loneliness, but out of which we can emerge with strength and maturity, and with something to *give*.

Perhaps I should state more definitely what the boy has to cope with. He becomes acutely conscious of the activity of his penis, of the sensitive way it responds to his secret thoughts. He is apt to be fascinated by it, and often the very thought or sight of it is enough to cause it to become erect. If he is the sort of boy whose sexual feelings normally turn towards girls (not all boys are like this) anything that reminds him of the sexuality of girls – the shape or movement of the female figure, the thought of touching or kissing a girl, even the sight of a girl's underclothing in a shop window – may cause an erection. This can be very disturbing. Often it leads to masturbation; the boy finds that he enjoys the sensation he feels when he touches his penis and he may carry the stimulation far enough to produce an orgasm, with the emission of seminal fluid. It is unlikely that this will happen without producing a strong sense of guilt. As I have shown already, this sort of guilt can be eased – though only superficially – by taking the activity into the group. The boy does it in the presence of others, all of whom may do the same. Although it may seem to ease the situation it is not really a satisfactory way; and the ultimate state may be more unhappy.

There are still many adults who look upon this with horror; either they must have very effectively forgotten their own youth or they must still feel a deep sense of guilt about it. Some fathers, even in these 'enlightened' times, threaten their sons with punishment. I have even seen a boarding-school in which threatening and lying notices were put up in the lavatories in the expectation of suppressing masturbation. They were lying notices because they stated that physical or mental disease would result. If any of the boys in that school became mentally unbalanced it was because of the notices not because of the masturbation. It has been emphasized in book after book by doctors and other specialists that the physical act does no harm. It is true that the boy would be tired and washed out if he did it often, but nothing more.

If there are bad results, for instance considerable anxiety, inability to get on with work, or to face parents and members of the other sex, it is because the boy has been unnecessarily frightened by it, because he has picked up some nonsensical idea of 'pollution', or because some misguided person has been getting at him with ideas about 'purity'. In my youth this latter activity was widespread and did very great harm. I shall shortly have more to say about this.

Boys should be assured that most of their fellows pass through this phase, that nearly all fathers have been through it and that it happens to girls and women too, though to a lesser extent. Doctors who specialize in the knowledge of sexual and mental development regard it as a *normal* experience, part of growing up sexually. All the same it is not a phase to get stuck in, and boys occasionally need to be helped out of it by talking the matter over with an adult. The mere fact of discovering that they can share the problem with an adult without embarrassment is itself a help. If a boy remains fixed in this stage, he is, so to speak, fixed in a condition of making love to himself, putting himself right in the middle of the sexual picture. Making love should be a way of reaching intimacy with another person, with its resulting enrichment of experience. So we all need to learn to turn our love outwards, away from ourselves – so that the *other* person is in the middle of the picture. There's no slick way of making this happen, but to be at ease about it instead of anxious, and to keep up your interest in other people, are the first steps in a process which will probably happen without your noticing it. You must *not* let it shut you off from girls or your parents. The idea that girls are specially 'pure' creatures often creates a severe difficulty – the thought that the wonderful girl whom you are going to meet in the future would be disgusted if she knew! Boys should know that girls have a generous capacity for accepting and understanding the physical side of life, and they are by no means free from the problem themselves.

Although I have said above that there are no bad results

from masturbation in itself I don't want to give the impression that it should be taken lightly, that the interest should be shared with other boys and indulged publicly, or that it should be indulged privately to whatever extent the boy desires. It is a normal impulse, but no normal impulse should be allowed to run away with us. All impulses have to be controlled and disciplined. This impulse is one that hasn't any permanent value and the sooner it is transformed into an outward-looking interest the better. This calls for some effort on the part of the boy. For some boys it becomes a deep preoccupation, and such boys need help urgently. I am thinking of the boy whose life seems to be going wrong, whose school work is poor, and who can't find any constructive interests to satisfy him. In these circumstances there is a strong temptation to turn more and more to masturbation, and this makes it even more difficult to give attention to active and outward pursuits. It's the job of adults to guess what is happening to such a boy and offer him help; if the boy himself can find a moment of courage to go and seek help, so much the better.

After reaching puberty boys begin to have 'wet dreams', which, like masturbation, are worrying to some. The penis becomes erect during sleep and at the end of a fantastic dream there is an orgasm, so that the boy wakes up to find the seminal fluid on his pyjamas. Although this sort of thing is quite unavoidable, many boys feel guilty about it. The dream is fantastic in the sense that the boy dreams that he is doing something which far exceeds anything he would in fact do – but which resembles in a vivid and exaggerated form, his daytime imaginings. It usually involves nakedness in public, urinating, or making sexual attempts upon some female person, probably not one who would ever enter his daydreams. The only thing to do about these experiences is to laugh them away, quietly, to yourself. There is absolutely no reason for anxiety or guilt. We've all had them, but they tend to cease when men become sexually satisfied. If the dream is shocking, it is no reflection on you. Its content comes up from 'down below' – the unconscious part of the mind which contains pretty nearly everything imaginable and more. You are not responsible for it – not in the way that you are responsible for what you deliberately and consciously do.

Oh – say you – but some of the things I imagine in my daydreams are pretty awful! They make me feel guilty, and they are conscious and deliberate! Yes, I know what you are thinking about. But here again the experience is universal. All human beings have these 'fantasies', as they are called. It is especially impossible to avoid them during the period when you are waiting – the many years during which you must do without sexual experience although your body is ready for it. You will perhaps never be quite free from them all your life. You must bear some responsibility, however. It is possible to let this sort of day-dreaming take hold of you so that in the end it becomes dominating and shuts you out from real life and real human contacts. Real human contacts, real interest in, and concern for, your friends will help you to control them. If there is one approach that is utterly useless – often indeed harmful – it is the 'purity' approach. This definitely states that it is your responsibility to shut out all impure and unclean thoughts from your mind, and that if you do not do so you are in a state of sin. This is not merely nonsense, it is cruelty, and cruelty to children. If a boy takes it seriously he is torn in two, detesting half of himself, an inevitable and normal part of himself. There is a widely used booklet in preparation for confirmation into the Church of England – it is thirty years old and ought to have been withdrawn long ago – in which there is a page and a half of cruel and suggestive writing, all about purity. I say suggestive, because nowhere does it say what 'Impurity' is. It simply says 'Your conscience will tell you'. Knowing how worried sensitive boys can become about their sexual thoughts I can say that this is the most cruel and unchristian part of the whole statement. I'm not making an attack on the Church of England; there are many people in the Church who feel as I do and would be just as angry about this way of approaching young people. But there is a serious danger to religion itself in all this. I remember that among my school-fellows there were a few who were driven to be unnaturally 'pious' by this approach. They were literally scared into being religious; and their religion, as a result, was a poor caricature of the real thing. Genuine religion grows out of the positive impulse of love and it cannot be based on fear. Moreover, if all that is in human nature was put there by God, it is not our task to stamp it out, but to make it serve love.

This brings me to what I think is the really helpful approach – the one that marriage has revealed to so many of us. All the content of your sexual thoughts can be taken into a loving relationship and made *good* there. Many of the actions you dream of, which perhaps shock you and are the sort of actions described as 'impure', you will some day *do* with someone you love, and they will be completely free from guilt. All sorts of things happen between people who love each other, accompanied by all sorts of feelings, from the most grave to the most hilarious, and they are all good because they are made good by a loving intimacy. Your job, then, is not to try to destroy part of yourself – this highly imaginative dreaming part – but to keep it within reasonable bounds, be patient with it, don't get into a state of hating yourself or despising yourself, and wait – wait until it can be released into the right relationship.

At this point I want to try to answer the question I put at the beginning of this section: What is sex for? Apart from the obvious purpose of producing babies, I would say that it is for the deepening of love and friendship. Love and friendship are not primarily sexual; it is obvious that deep feelings and personal intimacy can exist between people who are not conscious of anything sexual in their relationship, between for instance one man and another, one woman and another. But consider your friendship with a girl; suppose that at first it has nothing flirtatious about it but is a relationship of mutual respect, concerned with mutual interests and exchange of ideas. Then, if sexual attraction and love-making come into it at a later stage, the friendship will be taken to a much deeper level. In a love-relationship that has its roots in friendship there is a very strong impulse in each of the two partners to expose himself or herself completely to the other, not just physically, but personally. Each wants the other to know all about him, to know all his hopes, his ambitions and ideals, his interests, his strength – and also his fears and his weaknesses. There need be nothing held back. To be like that to another person is a very great freedom. That is what sex does to what begins as a friendship.

Young people are usually very conscious of isolation. As Erich Fromm has pointed out in his *Art of Loving*, everyone's greatest necessity is to overcome the feeling of isolation, of being shut off and alone. This comes before any need for sex. We need friendship, all of us, desperately. It is possible to have it without sex; and that is why many people are able to go happily through life without 'having sex'. They find companionship and love in other ways. But for most of us sex is the experience that takes us into the depths of friendship and away from isolation. But note what comes first – friendship. Again as Erich Fromm points out, there is a strong tendency for people to think that they will get rid of their sense of isolation when they find the right partner for their sexual life; sex will destroy the feeling of being alone in the world. In fact that doesn't work. Many people enter marriage and after the first excitements they are disappointed. They live and sleep and converse with another person, but are still alone in spirit. Before marriage they had learnt nothing about friendship, and marriage couldn't create it. Sex in itself is wild, primitive, unthinking, overwhelming. If there isn't already something sensitive and thoughtful between the partners, sex may make it even more difficult for them to see and understand each other's needs. Sex can't even create tenderness, though all the romances we read and hear about conspire to make us think that it can. On the other hand, sexual intimacy can provide a wonderful experience, an opening up of a new world, for people who *already* have a capacity for tenderness, who have already felt tenderness and compassion for those among their everyday friends who were in need of understanding and sympathy.

The foregoing should give you some idea as to what you can do during the long period of waiting that you may have to endure before complete sexual experience, such as comes to you through marriage. You can make it a time when you learn to enjoy and understand other people, when you develop an awareness of other people's needs at a deeper level and a generosity towards them. After that you will be ready for sexual experience.

7

HER BODY

IF you take a quick glance over the bookstall in a large stationer's or at a railway station, one fact is certain to strike you – the extensive publicity given to the body of the human female. There are the magazines directed particularly to servicemen, clubmen, hearty sportsmen, and similar types, hinting or definitely saying that they are for the private view of men, which of course means that they are largely concerned with sex in general, and women's bodies in particular. A general characteristic is the exaggeration of the breasts in all the illustrations, and the scanty covering of these and the genital parts. The wisps of clothing are intended to draw special attention to these parts and to suggest the excitement that would ensue if the covering were removed. Lavish magazines, expensively produced and with enormous circulations, pander to women's interest in their own bodies, illustrating every detail of their overwear and underwear, casting over all a glamorous and romantic aura . . . until you turn to the page where there is a discreet advertisement discussing menstruation and the sanitary problems that it involves. Boys often turn to these magazines when their mothers and sisters go out of the room and hurriedly replace them when footsteps are heard returning.

There are many influences in modern civilization conspiring to prevent a boy from being at ease about sex and about the bodies of girls. The effect of these magazines, of pin-ups, leg-shows, and strip-tease, is to encourage an obsessive interest in sex, an interest far beyond what is 'natural' to us. Mr C. S. Lewis, in an excellent chapter on Sexual Morality in his book *Mere Christianity*, asks what would be the effect of doing a strip-tease act, not with a girl's body but with a mutton chop. It would be possible, given the same extensive and continuous publicity as is given to sex, to make the people of this country so obsessed with mutton chops that the appetite for them became grossly exaggerated and distorted. Advertisement and propaganda are in fact doing this sort of thing to us all the time, to make us buy the things that other people want to sell. Our sexual impulses are deeper and stronger than most of our other impulses and so the temptation to exaggerate and distort is greater.

The breezy, happy-go-lucky boy finds his way through all the influences and exhibitions I have mentioned with jokes and laughter; but the more sensitive boy goes through a great deal of pain and bewilderment. He can't take references to sexual matters superficially; there is much more that he wants to know, and the more he searches for the truth about sex the more he becomes divided about it. He knows there is much more to a girl than just a body, but a casual glance at an advertisement for brassières may produce in him a state of sexual excitement. He feels guilty, because the interest is so physical and specific, and because he inherits from the society into which we are all born a long-established guilt-feeling about sex.

I want to try to dissipate in this chapter some of the guilt and discomfort that such a boy feels about his interest in a girl's body. The interest is completely normal and natural and any boy who did not feel it would be most unusual. We who are grown up have all known the interest, and it remains throughout life.

There's no doubt that the sexual forces which are in us as part of our nature are very strong, so strong that they can override our wisdom, deeply disturb our lives, and damage our personal relationships. But we should be better able to direct and control these forces within us if the influences at work on us from outside were more wholesome. Perhaps, however, in this respect sex is not very different from the rest of life's experiences. The world is full of good and evil and we can hope to achieve mastery of our circumstances only if we are prepared to make the effort to sort them out.

If we are not to become the victims of the ever-present evil, we must become aware of what the newspapers, the magazines, the films, and the pin-ups are doing to us. In the last forty years there has been an enormous increase in the publicity given to the female body, much of it daring, suggestive, provoking, enticing, and some of it plainly ridiculous. Not even our most respectable Sunday papers can remain untouched by the corset merchants. At the same time nakedness is considered to be wrong or indecent by those with conventional 'moral' attitudes. I put that word in inverted commas because I consider that the conventional attitudes I have in mind have nothing to do with true morality or integrity. Conventional morality has always considered nakedness improper, and even sinful, and in the tension created between this attitude and the publicity given to semi-nakedness, it is not surprising that the sight of a girl in a bikini has a powerful effect on an adolescent boy. If that boy could know what a naked girl really looks like, and could enjoy her beauty in wholesome circumstances, then the suggestiveness of a bikini would become to him absurd and stupid.

The sad result of the way the world upsets the attitudes of young people is that it encourages a divided feeling about sex and about people. It ought to be possible for a young man to see a girl naked and to enjoy her nakedness without any sense of guilt, accepting it not just as the nakedness of a female body, but as something that is part of her personality and that arouses respect for her as a whole person. There are countries in which the taboo on nakedness is not so strong as it is here. In Britain we have an inheritance of prudery that is very difficult to shake off, and one of the evidences of this is in the pretence that women have no pubic hair. It is possible for a boy to grow far into adolescence without being aware that girls are acquiring it in the same place as he is. Paintings and sculpture in art galleries are devoid of it. The most ludicrous pretence is that shown in photographs; 'nudes' are a popular item in photographic magazines, but it is often painfully evident where the negative or print has been tampered with to remove the hair.

Here is what Eric Gill had to say about it. Eric Gill was an artist, a sculptor, and an engraver, and he designed some of the most beautiful type used by printers. He was a deeply religious man, a Catholic, but free from the irrational fears that often accompany religion. He gives one the impression of being wholesome right through. He published two books of nudes, one of drawings and the other of engravings, and they are perhaps the frankest nudes published in this country. No attempt is made to get the model into conventionally modest poses – the poses in which the genital parts are obscured and therefore, of course, drawn attention to.

In a preface he writes:

We are creatures who know and will and love. What do we know and will and love? Whatever else may be said, we know and desire and love one another in a physical way. There is no escape from this and no denying it. Does anyone want to escape and deny? Perhaps the Buddhists want to escape; perhaps the Puritans would deny. But the rest of us accept the fact and are glad.

Drawings of the nude, therefore, have a special place in human affairs and a special veneration, and as human life is not all a matter of tears and sighs, but also, and equally and more importantly, a matter of laughter, there is naturally a comic side to all this. Don't let's be too solemn about it. Hair on the belly is certainly becoming but it is also very amusing – quite as amusing as hair on the head. Man is matter and spirit, both real and both good, and the funny is certainly part of the good. The human body is in fact a good joke – let us take it so.

In another preface:

With reference to those parts of the body which, because of their intimate conjunction with organs of drainage, suffer an opprobrium both unwarranted and psychologically dangerous, I think much trouble and misunderstanding can be avoided if we observe the world of flowers. Exactly as 'roses and lilies fair on a lawn' display the sexual parts of the rose and the lily, so, in literal fact, *our* sexual parts are *our* flowers, and that is a decent and salutary and sweetening way in which to regard them.

You will realize, from my approval of what Eric Gill has written, that I do not consider that in order to be at peace about nakedness and the body we need to be in a solemnly reverential state of mind. Eric Gill was a supremely reverent man, but, as you see, his enjoyment of beauty included gaiety and humour. However young you are, you will have encountered funny stories about sex and the body, and you may be wondering how the humour that I believe to be good differs from the humour of the dirty story. I think it is that the dirty story treats of the body as though it were just a vehicle for the sexual parts, as though it were a not very important framework to which the sexual organs were attached. So the teller of dirty stories doesn't think of the body as a whole; its beauty and its unity are missing.

I can illustrate this best by referring to the male body. Can anyone deny that the penis is a comical organ? Of course it is; it is amusing on a boy baby, as any normal mother will readily admit, and it remains comical throughout life. If you think of it alone, apart from the body, this comical quality degenerates into something nasty; but if you see it as part of a fine man's or boy's body, it will take its place in the dignity of the whole. In Florence there is a magnificent and beautiful statue of the boy David, by Michelangelo. The body is complete, nothing is left out. Its beauty and dignity are so great that any sexual reference to its nakedness would be utterly out of place.

Most boys in their teens spend a great deal of time thinking about a girl's body, but few have any opportunity to see it in circumstances that are wholesome. Some snatch opportunities in circumstances that are definitely unfortunate, when the experience is spoilt by furtiveness, guilt, ribaldry, or coarseness. Many have no opportunity and you, the reader, may be one of these. What are you to do then? First, accept your desire as normal; then try to sort out the various interests that arise from it. You will be driven to find a substitute for the real experience; you will turn to the pages of magazines in which nearly naked bodies are exhibited, you will be specially interested in works of art concerned with the naked body, or with photographic records of it. Don't feel there is anything wrong about this, but try to be *discriminating*. When you have stopped feeling guilty about your interest, or stopped making a dirty joke of it, then begin to think about the different qualities of these representations. Compare the partially naked with the wholly naked, and ask yourself what is the *intention* behind the picture or photograph. What are the different effects on you? What did the artist, the photographer, the newspaper editor want you to feel?

A real artist is not primarily concerned with what you feel when you look at his picture; he is concerned with being truthful in portraying what *he* sees and feels. You may be able to enjoy his work by entering into the truth and sincerity of his feeling. A good photographer may work in the same way. But another, and particularly the newspaper editor, may have definite designs on you. He wants to use you. He must stimulate you because he must sell his paper. Try to be keenly aware of the way books, the press, films, and pictures tend to influence you. Hold them off; do not buy sexy papers just because it is the habit of men to do it. Insist on being an individual and making your own judgements. Don't be a herd-man, a follower of the crowd, the simpleton out of whom the newspaper men and the pulp-magazine proprietors make their profit.

Need I point out the nature of the stimulation? I have already hinted at it. The skimpy bra, the very brief briefs, are intended to draw your interest to the sexual parts only, to lead your thoughts away from the whole body and the person whose body it is, to the breasts, the pubic hair, and the vagina, as though these were all that a woman consisted of, or existed for. I am not often inclined to moralize about sex, but I think it is well to consider what is the fundamental evil in sexual conduct and thinking. I would say that it is the dividing off of the sexual parts and sexual activity from the rest of the body and especially from the *person*. It leads to a destruction of the real meaning of sex, and it encourages conduct in which a person is *used* for sexual purposes. But what do I mean by a *person*? I mean an actual individual with a particular name, with a past and a future, with particular qualities and feelings, somebody real, as real as your friends or members of your family. If you think of sex as part of a person's wholeness, you won't want sex experience with just a girl's body; it will matter supremely who that girl is.

Often in a so-called love-affair the boy is preoccupied with getting at the girl's sexual parts – petting – but has little interest in her personality or general qualities. This is destructive; sex, which can be lovely and wholly guiltless when it belongs to a deepening friendship, simply 'goes bad' when it is indulged separately, and brings no lasting satisfaction.

I might emphasize what the effect of the wrong attitude is by referring to what one of my pupils, a girl of 18, told me after she had voyaged to India alone to see her father. When I asked her whether she had enjoyed the voyage, she answered more or less in the affirmative, but with a qualification. She had been educated at a boarding-school, a co-education one, where the boys, though rough-and-tumble as most boys are, knew and liked her as a person. On the ship she met something different. 'The men', she said, 'undressed me with their eyes. I was not a person, I was just a body.' It is important to note that these were not bad men; they were just – men.

I have suggested that your interest in the pictures of the female body is a substitute for the real experience, and it may be that you will have to be content with substitutes until you are fully adult and intimately in love or married. Well, be patient; the good is well worth waiting for, and if in the meantime you have developed good taste by learning to discriminate, the real thing when it comes to you will be overwhelmingly satisfying and meaningful. It may prove to be one of the most moving experiences in your whole life. But if instead you have surrounded yourself with suggestive pin-ups and titivated your sexual appetite with cheap magazines, then you will have to get rid of a bad taste in the mouth before you can know the good in all its sweetness.

If you become discriminating about the substitutes, the photographs and pictures, you will also begin to be discriminating about the personal qualities of the girls you know. When you marry, you will marry a person, not just a face or a figure, and the kind of person you marry is in the long run more enduring than the pretty face or appealing figure. Learn to read character in face or behaviour. The girl who is always drawing attention to her looks may not be a warm-hearted, unselfish, and generous person who is good to live with.

It may seem to be implied in some of the statements I have made that it is good for young people to see each other naked. I believe it is, especially when they are prepared for it by a sane upbringing and a good relationship with their parents. But there are dangers. The introduction of the wrong attitude by one or other of the people concerned may turn the experience from something good into something horrid. There is in all of us a lot of evil, and we often walk nearer to a precipice than we know. Among friends who are sensitive to what they are doing, the experience can be spontaneous, care-free, and delightful; but when people begin to go bad in a group they go faster than in any other circumstances. I would add, too, that it is never wise for two people of opposite sexes to be naked together alone, unless they are already deeply committed to each other in engagement or marriage. I have not said that it is *wrong*, but that it is not *wise*. Customary moral judgements are rarely helpful; you perhaps call them 'stuffy' and want to ignore them; but it *is* important to govern our behaviour by knowing our own nature, knowing just how far we can in fact control our impulses. Two people – almost any two – together in intimate circumstances are easily aroused to strong sexual desires, and there soon comes a point beyond which control is extremely difficult. If it is not desirable that two young people should become sexually intimate, then it is most important that they should avoid a situation in which 'nature' takes charge and impels them towards mating. Never allow yourself to over-estimate your powers of control. We are all of us, old and young alike, less able to control ourselves than we think we are.

Lest anything I have said about bad attitudes and about the need for wholeness and beauty in sex should make it seem that I am moving towards a solemn attitude, I want to emphasize again that the state of mind in which sex is part of the whole personal relationship is one that is reverent but also full of gaiety and humour. I want to dissociate myself from the pseudo-religious attitude which seems to hold that we can make sex good only by making it pious. The naked body of the woman we love does inspire reverence, but reverence does not necessarily imply a long face. Indeed it is often in a reflective moment during an experience of the greatest gaiety and care-free enjoyment that we realize that what we enjoy is a gift of God. You may feel guilty about the jokes you and your friends make about sexual aspects of the body, male or female, and with one part of yourself you may look forward to a time when you will stop doing things that make you feel guilty. But you need not think that this will have to happen by your renouncing the humour, nor even what one might call the anatomical interest. In a good love relationship these things remain as strong as ever, but their quality changes and all the guilt falls away. You will not need to leave anything behind you when you go into such a marriage; you will be able to take it all with you and find it good.

I said 'into such a marriage', and I have to recognize that all marriages are not of this sort. In some, deeply-rooted prejudices and fears in one or both partners make this impossible to achieve. But it is the purpose of this book to help young people to prepare themselves for a better sort of marriage than is usually achieved.

There is another side to this question of the boy's feeling

about a girl's body that I have not yet mentioned. Many boys have an idealistic feeling about a girl's body, even though they may be tempted to make dirty jokes about it in a gang. It may be difficult for them to harmonize the idealistic feeling with the awareness of what happens regularly in a girl's body. I can remember so clearly the way menstruation was talked about among my fellow-pupils in the grammar school. Some boys were thoroughly coarse about it. The more sensitive listened in a fascinated sort of way, became worried, and tended to think of menstruation as something secret and nasty, something that one had to thrust out of mind if one wanted to think of a girl as a delicate and beautiful creature or even as lovable.

This need not happen if the minds of boys and girls are properly prepared. The fear of menstruation is indeed very primitive and is found well established in the terrors and taboos of primitive peoples. Savage cultures, both those existing far in the past and some in the present, are full of the fear of the menstruating girl. Sometimes they insist on cruelly shutting her away, imposing a virtual imprisonment, for long periods of time. The many references to 'uncleanness' and 'cleansing' in the early books of the Bible have probably done much harm to the attitude of young people. However civilized we claim to be, we are never quite free from these primitive fears; but the fear is one that can be eradicated by sensible upbringing. I know from many years' experience as an educator that boys who are properly told about the body and its functions, who are educated with girls and whose friendships with them are wholesome, can accept without difficulty the fact of menstruation. They can be well aware why a girl has sometimes to excuse herself from swimming and accept this without more than a passing thought.

Both boys and girls have to learn to accept their bodies in a complete way, and try to get away from the idealism that seeks to forget part of its physical functions. We all have to use lavatories; both males and females have to discharge various sorts of waste matter. The one thing we can do about it is to be hygienic and keep ourselves clean and fresh by frequent washing.* In health the skin has a lovely quality; its responsiveness is always a delight, it looks and feels good, and it smells good if kept clean, even without the help of scent.

On the whole a girl accepts the physical side more readily than a boy does. She has to, indeed, otherwise life would be impossible for her. As I have indicated elsewhere, a boy may become disturbed by the developments in his body when he begins to become a man; the behaviour of his penis may alarm him with its apparent power, seeming almost independent of him. He may feel in a way divided from his body because of this. But to a girl – if she has been wisely and fearlessly prepared by her mother – the development of her childish body into that of a woman is a reason for great pride and contentment. The growth of the breasts and the pubic hair is a source of great satisfaction to her. One young woman, speaking of this phase in her life, said: 'I was delighted, thrilled; it just couldn't happen fast enough!' But I remember from my schooldays that it is just at such a time that boys begin to notice what is happening and to make ribald comments, calling attention to it in a way that disgusts the girls and makes them self-conscious and disturbed about what should be wholly a matter of delight. They are thus prevented from enjoying their developing womanhood, as is their right. The special difficulty here is that the boys who do this, though they may be of the same age as the girls, are less mature and at a heedless, insensitive stage. The difficulty can be got over, at least in part, if there is a good, considerate attitude in the older boys, for these can provide the girls with reassurance and perhaps curb the verbal assaults of the younger ones.

* It should be said that boys and men ought to keep up as high a standard of cleanliness in their own persons as they expect of their girl friends and their womenfolk. Women are extraordinarily tolerant of dirtiness and smelliness in the men they love, but such tolerance ought not to be necessary.

8

PERSONS

THROUGHOUT this book you will find me often using the word *personal*. I refer to a personal relationship as something distinct from a physical relationship, a romantic relationship, or a functional relationship. It is very important to try to understand what is meant by the word personal and what we mean when we think of human beings as persons.

It may be best to start by saying what is *not* personal, what the other relationships are. Take the functional. A function is a job that a human being is trained to do or a machine is designed to do. When I refer to a man as a *worker* I am thinking of him functionally. So I can talk about 'the workers' as a mass of people who have a function and be quite uninterested in *who* each worker is. They are simply beings whose function is to work. Now the physical. When I refer to a man as a 'male' and a woman as a 'female', I am thinking of them purely in their physical relationship. Incidentally you should observe that each is necessary to the definition of the other. If there were no females the word 'male' would be meaningless. Each has organs needed by the other; the female has a vagina and uterus for the reception of sperm and for the nourishment of a foetus, breasts for the feeding of a baby after birth. The male has testicles and a penis with which he can fertilize the female. The male has a strong impulse to put his penis into the female and the female has a strong desire that he should do so. We can talk about males and females in this way without implying that we are in any way interested in *who* each male is, *who* each female is. If you put male and female rabbits together, they behave as males and females, and their relationship is a physical one; they mate without any sensitive discrimination and any female will do for any male.

What about the romantic? Isn't that personal? Isn't it

89

very much concerned with a particular boy or girl? Let's look at one of these pulp-paper strip-cartoon stories; they are definitely called 'romantic'. Look at the faces of all the girls. Is there much difference between them? Is there much difference between the men? Haven't they all been drawn by an artist(!) who has simply one or two *types* in mind? Do you think that this artist would be the man to paint portraits of the members of your family and put into those portraits the distinctive personalities of these people you know so well? No, you must realize that the romantic story is not concerned with the particular individual people to whom the events happen. It doesn't matter *who* they are. Yet countless young people read them and moon over them, the intelligent as well as the dull. Consider your own feelings as you read – or look. I think you will find that it is not individuals you are interested in but feelings, your *own* feelings. When the square-jawed young man at last gets the girl he has been fighting for and crushes his lips on to hers, you tend to identify yourself with that young man and feel as he feels. Your tastes may however be a little above these strip-cartoons. But precisely the same thing may happen when you half-ashamedly pick up a woman's magazine and read the stories therein. Not so crude but just as romantic. Many of these stories are written to a formula laid down by a correspondence course run by a school for aspiring authors. Such 'schools' know what stirs the public and they tell their pupils what to write.

Perhaps you don't read even women's magazines. But you do read novels. Think of some novel in which the writer steps aside now and then to describe very carefully the distinctive appearance and underlying character of one of his men or women. Don't you find yourself tending to skip this? You want to get on with the events, what happens to the people, what fears, impulses, temptations surge through their breasts. Further, you have dreams. In some of them you may imagine yourself performing wonderful feats of courage, cleverness in argument, success in scholarship, or the courting of charming girls. In these dreams you are not concerned with what you really are but with an emotional picture of what you would like to be. In other dreams you picture the girl you are in love with, or the imaginary girl you want to meet some day. You invest her with various interesting, attractive, or lovable qualities so that you may have the feelings about her that you want to have.

Now all these activities I describe as romantic. But I must put in at this point that I am not using the word as it is used in the history of music and literature – in for instance the phrase 'the Romantic Movement'. I am using it in the everyday sense. We are all romantic in this sense. We never quite cease to see ourselves on a stage of our making, though the rude shocks to our self-esteem that life gives us make us more capable as time goes on of laughing at our romantic thoughts. The awful danger to the young is that of projecting their romantic wishes on to real people, so that they see them as they would like them to be, not as they really are. A very ordinary girl may be seen as a possessor of all the virtues and charm in the world by a boy who is hungry for love. A girl who has become romantically worked up about a film star may fail to see the good qualities that really exist in a plain boy friend and may turn from him to a man more dashing in appearance but without real qualities. A romantic relationship is not a real relationship between people; it is essentially an attachment to a notion, a stock conception, a feeling. The other person is just a convenient peg on which to hang the romantic picture.

People who reject the romantic impulse in the crude form I have described sometimes adopt something just as romantic but masquerading under a more respectable name: idealism. These people look for the 'ideal partner' and reject ordinary people because they are not good enough. They don't use other people as a peg; they reject them altogether. For them the very possession of an ideal implies a perpetual criticism of real people.

It should be clear that I have been leading up to an explanation of personal relationship as a relationship between people who know each other for what they really are, virtues and faults together, and who happily accept each other on this basis. For each one the other is a distinct individual, with a particular and distinct set of qualities, good and bad, making up a certain whole pattern, a unity called Bill or Mary or John or Alfred. But although each may recognize and accept the other's faults, he does not spend his time sorting out and listing them; he knows them, accepts them, lets them slide into the back of his mind, and just enjoys being with his friend. Men normally accept each other as friends in this way. If men and women could do the same, there would be much less trouble between them after marriage.

However, I am not at the moment concerned with what happens after marriage, but with what boys and girls, men and women, can do before it. This is what they can do. They can look into their thoughts and urges and recognize where romantic and idealistic notions are leading them away from real people. They can begin to watch what the cinema, T.V., the magazines, and the newspapers are tending to do to their feelings and desires. They can make a deliberate attempt to see their friends as they really are, not trying to sort out faults in an uncharitable way, but seeing them as fellow human beings. Each boy whom I ask to do this is himself as chock full of faults as most boys, so if he recognizes faults in other boys or in girls, he should do so clearly but humbly, being prepared to look into himself as he looks into them, and perhaps being able finally to say: 'This is life; we are all in it together, we are all made of the same stuff and we can offer each other what each of us in our weakness and loneliness needs – friendship.'

What you find if you adopt this attitude to life and friendship is that when you stop using other people as pegs they are profoundly *interesting*. Life becomes extraordinarily rich and satisfying. You become glad that you are in this world, you don't long for any other. You stop being lonely because other people become real to you. You no longer walk about in a world peopled by images of your own making. This may be difficult for you to understand at first, perhaps because like most people you have got into the idealistic habit of thinking what a much nicer world this would be if everybody were more nearly perfect. There is altogether too much encouragement to judge other people in terms of 'good' and 'bad' instead of feeling compassion for them and enjoying their company. What I mean by compassion is a deep sort of sympathy based upon a realization that the other person, like you, is up against life's problems, probably feeling in private that he is not quite big enough, wise enough, or strong enough to cope with it all.

Have you ever thought what it is that really holds people together in friendship? Probably not. Boys accept friendship without thinking much about it. For them friendship is so often based on the enjoyment together of some outside interest – cars or sport or mountains or photography. They don't stop and ask: *why do we like each other?* In adult life when severe difficulties have to be faced, friendship is often sorely tried. The interesting thing to me is that often failure and disaster hold people together more firmly than does success. It is certainly true of nations. The moment when a group of nations achieves victory is the moment when they begin to quarrel among themselves; but nations experiencing a common disaster grow together. I want to take this a little deeper. I think that people are often held together in love by the awareness of their common weakness and failure. When we have triumphed in some struggle we begin to get illusions about ourselves and imagine ourselves bigger and stronger than we are. But two people in trouble know each other in truth, in common humanity.

So we need not fear that having faults or weaknesses will necessarily make a lasting love-relationship impossible. But having illusions – about yourself or your partner – is very likely to make it impossible. The word 'disillusioned' has an unpleasant sound about it, as though it were something we ought never to feel. In fact it is a very good state to be in. We usually take it to mean the same as 'bitterly disappointed', but it simply means 'no longer believing things that are not true'. If we have ceased to believe things that are not true we are wiser – and should therefore be stronger – than we were before. As I have said or implied already, people are so much more lovable when we cease to see them in an untrue way and accept them as plainly human.

Marriage, or any intimate friendship that involves facing life together, does suffer and has to suffer strains. Some writers have been more than disillusioned, in fact cynical, about marriage because of this. A French writer once wrote that love could not possibly survive the strains of continued living together because each would have to put up with the physically unpleasing things that happen to human bodies – to the body of the other. He was presumably thinking of wind, diarrhoea, the odours of disease, vomiting, the smell of sweat – all things that happen to women just as they do to men, and all exceedingly unromantic. But can't love stand this sort of thing? Did your mother love you any the less for having to cope with your filthy clothes, your smelly socks, and your dirty body when you came in off the street? Would she have loved you more if you had always been immaculately clean? What the writer believed is perhaps much more the sort of thing a man would say than a woman. Romantic attitudes encourage men to think of girls as essentially fastidious, pure, scrupulously clean, and abhorring dirt and smells. In fact women have to cope much more than men do with the dirty side of life – with the sort of mess that is produced by our animal bodies. They cope with it in their babies, and birth itself is a messy business. They cope patiently with drunken husbands and the sickness they produce. They face up to all the problems of illness with extraordinary resource. As nurses in hospitals they cope with the revolting conditions of suppurating flesh and carry innumerable loaded bedpans; and while doing this they can continue to express affection and tenderness for the patients who produce the mess and whose bodies are anything but lovable. Among medical students watching their first operations it is more often the men who faint than the women.

Yes, the romantic conception of love is just one great lie.

Real love, the love that is based upon a personal relationship, is the love that holds two people together 'for better for worse, for richer for poorer, in sickness and in health' and, one might add, in moments of failure, wretchedness, and despair.

I began this chapter by saying that I wanted to make clear the difference between a personal relationship on the one hand and functional, physical, romantic relationships on the other. I realize that I have not considered whether a man and a woman can be brought to a sexual experience with a functional relationship in mind to begin with. Of course they can. For the sake of clear thinking I have had to make a distinction between the physical, the functional, and the personal type of relationship. But a particular instance will never be purely one of these, though one may predominate. Moreover the quality of a relationship may change in the course of time. In peasant communities a man may quite deliberately choose for a wife a woman who is physically strong and likely to bear him many sons and daughters to share the burden of farm work. Romantically-minded young people may not like this idea, but nevertheless it often works well. People who recognize that life is tough and that they've got to work strenuously together to meet its demands are in a better position to meet difficulties and crises than people who get married in order to satisfy romantic longings. Moreover, out of a partnership that is directed *outwards* – and farming is an outward direction of your energy – a deep and tolerant personal relationship can often grow.

It has its dangers, however. It could go the wrong way; the man could continue to *use* the woman more and more for the achievement of his purposes. He could make her little more than a domestic servant and a breeding animal, finally casting her aside and neglecting her when no longer of use for either of these purposes. There has to be at least the beginning of a personal relationship in all partnerships, just sufficient sensitiveness of spirit to begin to recognize what has to be sought for. When the romantic illusions have gone, when the woman recognizes that she is being *used* and rebels, when the man is accused of being weak under his handsome face, then that sensitiveness, if it exists, is the thing that will grow and save the partnership.

Sometimes there is little difference between the functional and the physical. Many young men quickly dispense with the romantic point of view, and begin to think of girls as objects for sexual use. They are to be played with, joked with, teased, and flattered – but with the ultimate and definite object of enticing them into bed. The young men may consider that they are giving the girls something in return for this use of them; they are giving them 'experience' or 'a bit of fun', but this takes nothing away from the fact that they are *using* them, often cynically. The object is not the satisfaction of a big romantic longing, but of a definite physical desire; there's nothing vague about it, they know exactly what they want and they are prepared to discard each girl in turn when another offers new opportunities for physical sensation.

A personal relationship has its own inherent morality, a morality that is not imposed by any rules from outside. In a relationship that is truly personal you simply *cannot* use the other person without being aware that you are destroying or denying something. Such a relationship has a self-corrective quality therefore that tends to restore the original good conditions after anything has gone temporarily wrong.

I haven't said all that can be said about the nature of personal relationships. The subject is an endless one, precisely because persons and our liking for them, our interest in them, and our enjoyment of them are endless in their variety, and there is no limit to the depth and the discoveries possible in a personal relationship.

9

MORALS

I WONDER what the word morals suggests to you? Some young people will think of morals with immediate respect, feeling that they are unlikely to be tempted to be immoral and certain that even if tempted they will be able to resist. Others may be impatient with morals and be inclined to say that they are 'mere conventions'. I am, of course, referring to sexual morals, not the morality that is concerned with general behaviour, and that would forbid such actions as stealing and fraud. Boys and girls in the early teens, if they think about sexual morality at all, are not likely to question it, because they have not yet reached a stage in which they want to do things that are in conflict with accepted morality. Most of them know, however, what is meant by morality – and by immorality. It is held to be immoral for sexual intercourse to take place between any two people who are not married; that is what one might call the main principle. Thus it is considered immoral for unmarried people to go to bed together, no matter whether they do so casually and irresponsibly or with every intention of marriage at a later date. It is immoral for a married person to have intercourse with some person other than the husband or wife; this is called adultery. There are many actions thought of as grossly immoral and some as criminally immoral. Seduction, which means the over-persuasion of someone into having intercourse, the breaking down of scruples and resistance by skilled love-making, is considered grossly immoral when the seduced person is adult, and criminal when he or she is a child. Rape, which is the term given to the action in which a woman is forced into intercourse without any consent from her at all, is a criminal action treated in court with almost as much severity as manslaughter. Homosexual acts – abnormal sexual acts between two persons of the same, not opposite, sex – are usually thought of as immoral, and when practised between males are criminal – though the Wolfenden Committee has recommended that consenting adults should not be liable to prosecution.

In addition to these actions that are thought of as definitely immoral, there are many half-way actions that would be considered equally immoral by a good many people, for instance: sexual stimulation, by petting, of a girl who is not really old enough for love-making, the showing off of the naked body in order to stimulate sexual interest or in such a way as to be 'indecent', or even love-play stopping short of intercourse between people, one of whom is married and the other not.

So wide is the variety of actions thought of as immoral by one person or another that it really is necessary to do some hard thinking about it, in order to find some better distinction, some deeper principle that will help you to decide what you ought not to do and what you can allow yourself to do. One of the really devastating criticisms to be made of the everyday idea of morality is that it almost takes for granted that once people are married, nothing they can do to each other is immoral. A man can force his wife to consent to intercourse when she does not want it; conventional morality does not condemn this, yet the same thing happening between a man and a woman not married to him might earn the man several years of imprisonment.

I must first say something briefly about the legal side. The law used to be much fiercer than it is now and there used to be many forms of sexual behaviour that were punishable. It no longer attempts to control or punish adultery, and it would not be in the least practicable to do so. But the law does protect children and women from having unpleasant and damaging experiences forced upon them. A sexual attempt on a child is an assault and punished as such, even though there may be no obvious brutality. Even when a girl has become physically mature at, say, fourteen it is not good for her to be placed in a sexual

situation in which she might willingly consent to intercourse; she is not mentally ready to make such decisions.
So it has been made an offence to have sexual intimacy with
a girl under the age of sixteen – the age of consent – no
matter what the circumstances.

I must add another few words about rape. Most of the
boys who read this book will be unable to imagine themselves in a situation in which they could possibly be guilty
of such a crime. But many of the young men sentenced in
court for rape are not criminal types. A man charged with
rape may have to face more bias in the jury than if he were
charged with some other offence. In English law a man
brought to court is supposed to be presumed innocent unless
he is proved guilty. I think it would be fair to say, however,
that in sexual offences, especially rape, the ordinary jury-
man is so shocked, and people in general are so frightened
by this manifestation of the destructive power of sex, that
there is a strong tendency to take the side of the girl at the
outset. Yet there are usually no witnesses of the event, there
is only the girl's word and she may well have led the boy
on until the last moment – the moment when he lost control.
I once listened to a case of precisely this sort, in which the
accused was a fresh-faced farm-boy who had joined the
army. He wasn't very intelligent and he just stood there in
the dock looking bewildered. He was given three years'
hard labour. Sentences might be less savage, but the law
must not be relaxed, for rape *is* a serious crime. It will,
however, always be difficult to apply the law with fairness.
For every case that is brought to court, there may be hundreds, of the doubtful sort I have described, that are never
disclosed, because the girls do not tell their parents.

This implies that any boy who plays around with a girl
of whose attitude he is not absolutely certain may later find
himself accused of a crime. Quite apart from the question
of whether conventional morality is right or wrong it would
be well for every young man to make it a rule that he should
not expect intercourse from a girl who does not unmistakably love him, moreover that he should not allow himself to

get into a situation in which his body begins to make ungovernable demands. Many of the instances of rape are the culmination of a larking, flirting, teasing relationship of short duration. The girl must not be blamed for enticing and then refusing, not *necessarily*, and certainly not if she is new to the experience of 'walking out'; girls often don't know what is coming until the last moment.

Should we accept the ordinary pattern of morality? Obviously we've got to go a good deal further than ordinary morality demands. I pointed out that this morality is not interested in what happens after marriage, that acts of cruelty can take place in marriage which are just as bad as any that happen outside it. As long as the couple appear outwardly respectable there is no accusation of immorality. This makes it necessary to distinguish between 'conventional morality' and 'true morality'. Now I am faced again with the inconvenience of language. The word 'morals' should, from its Latin derivation, *mores*, apply only to what is conventional or customary, and true morality is more concerned with ethics than with customs. Ethics is the word that covers the department of thought that tries to get down to the deepest levels in discussing how people ought to behave in a variety of situations. Nevertheless the idea of 'true morality' has come to stay, and I shall allow myself to use the term.

Conventional morality does to some extent arise out of true morality. A society may become disorganized and dissolute, in danger of complete destruction from within because its people are behaving without any regard for the consequences of their actions. A new understanding and a new faith may begin to grow up and people begin to pull themselves together, creating new standards of behaviour which they know will make for a healthy and enduring society. This is precisely what happened when Christianity began to grow up in the pagan world. The rules of conduct that arise in this kind of situation are felt to be good from within. But people begin to talk about them and say that other people ought to abide by them. So in the course of time they become rules that are applied from without, required authoritatively by the Church or even the government. They *may* still be good, but they no longer necessarily come from the heart, and those who are rebelliously inclined begin to question them.

I think we are in a condition, in this country and elsewhere in the world, in which sexual morality in its conventional form is inadequate, certainly inadequate in its appeal, and we must therefore try to get down to something more fundamental. Now I know that many young people are anti-religious, and you – the reader – may be one of them. If you are, don't put the book down at this point because you think I am going to try to convert you. I'm not. I recognize as clearly as anyone the cruelty, hatred, humbug, hypocrisy, deceit, corruption, and sheer devilry of which, in the name of the Christian Church, some of its members have been guilty in the last two thousand years. And nowhere has the cruelty and the Pharisaism of the Church and its members been more apparent than in their attitude to the problems of sex. But it is interesting to note that very many of the people who attack the Christian Church are at pains to point out how the Church has failed to follow the lead of its own founder, how the Church began to betray Jesus almost from the moment of its foundation. They usually imply, and often state, that they would have nothing but praise for the Church if only it were truly Christian. There is a very great deal that I would like to say about this but I must content myself with a few brief remarks to indicate my attitude. Although I feel strongly the truth of these criticisms of the Church – by which I mean all its sects together – I would not have the Church destroyed, because I think it preserves, in spite of its dreadful weaknesses, something supremely important. It has relevance to all that we do in life, and certainly relevance to sexual behaviour.

There's another point. All men and women, even those who pretend to be without principles, do recognize the value of certain standards and to some extent direct their lives in the light of them. It might be nothing more pretentious than a belief in good sportsmanship, in not hitting the other fellow while he's down. Even if we never think about these standards, we usually accept them in our daily lives, and the fact that we accept them makes it possible for society to hold together. To a very large extent the habits and standards that make society and community life possible are part of an attitude specially fostered by Christianity – an attitude that the pre-Christian world did not foster. Though we usually make a sharp distinction between Christianity and the Jewish religion, the quality of the Christianity that I am thinking of had its roots deep in the Jewish religious feeling that life must be a unity, lived with meaning and purpose. Under the surface of society, and behind the elaborate façade of the organized Church, what I call true Christianity has been quietly at work like yeast in dough. I think we owe much of our modern thought and aims to this unseen and unrecognized Christianity – our ideas of social justice, of integrity in politics, our concern for universal education, for humanity in the treatment of criminals, our care for the sick and aged, our efforts to achieve true equality for women. This is my view, and it can only be examined by careful historical study, for which there is no room here.

In the beginning Christianity did something quite definite about sex, something that was very necessary. The pagan world in which Christianity emerged two thousand years ago was a dark world – far darker than our own. It was a world, as Chesterton put it, 'coloured by dangerous and rapidly deteriorating passions; by natural passions becoming unnatural passions'. He goes on '. . . the effect of treating sex as only one innocent natural thing was that every other innocent natural thing became soaked and sodden with sex.'

Christianity rescued sex from depravity and obscenity by 'sanctifying' it, but that is not a good word to use nowadays. I would say, by making it an expression of a personal relationship at its deepest, and of a commitment. This was a tremendous service to humanity, and few people realize how much they owe to the Christian Church for the good use of sex. It has to be admitted that at the same time the Church continued to fear what it fought against and many of its members have so feared and distrusted the primitive in sex that their faith in the good expression of sex has hardly been apparent. Nevertheless I consider that we can reach a true morality by following a Christian argument.

Now I think we have something from which we can start in trying to find a true morality. It is respect for the *other person*. To put it another way: *thou shalt love thy neighbour as thyself*. That may strike you as a very strange thing to say to people who are in love with each other. Surely it is already implied in the love-situation? But is it? It would be quite safe to say that in the majority of love-situations it is definitely not. I have already said a good deal about the romantic situation, in which the man (or the woman as the case may be) uses the other as a mirror, in which he sees, not the girl but an image of something in his own mind. What often lies under the surface of what appears to be love can be seen when love is frustrated. One partner cannot fall in with the wishes of the other in something important. An angry reaction is provoked and far greater bitterness expressed than in an ordinary quarrel between two men. There is no underlying respect. This respect that I consider to be so essential includes a respect for the other person's – the girl's – integrity. The word integrity is used to indicate a person's wholeness – the way the personality fits together into a sound pattern. To love your neighbour as yourself, in this instance your girl friend, is to see her as an independent person standing in her own right, as real and definite and independently distinct as yourself, not a creature to be bent to your will, softly cajoled to fall in with your designs or to be disappointed with if she comes to her own conclusions. Your love for her and what you ask from her should not destroy any part of her integrity. People do not often think about their integrity, but 'conscience' is a sort of focal point of integrity; and usually to attack a girl's conscience, however gently, is to attack her integrity. If you want intercourse – or petting – and she believes that in the circumstances it would be wrong, you must not use your love or any other emotional means to persuade her. Nor should you use your superior powers of argument, for that is an emotional weapon too, just as definitely. She must come to it, if she comes to it at all, freely, in her own time, when she is ready in thought and feeling and able to take her full share of the responsibility. It is no use your saying 'I'll take the responsibility'; you cannot, except by depriving her of her status as a responsible human being.

There is another insidious argument that tends to destroy responsibility. 'But, darling, we love each other; what does anything else matter?' This is insidious because there is an element of truth in it. When people truly love each other they can bear great responsibilities together, they can face trouble and support each other through endless difficulties. But when the argument is used to waive conscience, to destroy scruples, to contract out of responsibility for actions, then it becomes untrue and its ultimate effect is the opposite.

Even if we put on one side the word love, we find that the word 'respect' can be equally misleading. It often happens that a man will express 'deep respect' for the girl he loves; but this respect proves as romantic and sentimental as 'love' can be, for in practice he assumes that he is the superior person, the one to make judgements and decisions, to decide the course of their life together. The woman has no effective place in their common life, the respect is bogus, and the situation immoral.

There is, of course, the time-honoured idea that in the courting situation the man pursues and the woman is pursued, that she is by nature reluctant but ready to be persuaded. It would seem then that the woman will always appear to have a conscience, but that it isn't real. In fact the whole idea is of only very limited application; it applies only to the superficial, playful aspect of love. It should never be acted upon in any situation of serious consequence. At such times it should be completely abandoned, love-making should stop, and the two should seek a decision with some measure of detachment and with every relevant factor in mind.

There's another argument I can imagine which might at first seem a bit difficult to meet. It would run like this, coming from the young man. 'I'm not one of your idealistic blokes; I don't know that I've got much of an opinion of myself. As for being a person, well I don't know quite *what* I am. Depends on my mood. Now, as for girls, I find a lot of them are like me. No high falutin notions, but they know how to enjoy themselves. They know the rules of the game, same as I do. They don't expect anything more from it than I do; no more, no less. We're equal and we won't make any claims on each other. A wink and a kiss and a cuddle – and we're in bed. Any harm done?'

Now it is quite true that there are many such girls – both at the street corner and in the university. You can have equality with them, at your own level. You don't love – value and respect – yourself any more than you do the girl. It seems, then, that to love your neighbour as yourself is not enough, and this is indeed where the argument fails. As human beings our vision and our responsibility have to go beyond every immediate situation, otherwise the human race would never have raised itself above the animal level. The girl you go to bed with has a future, or should have. What will this *do to her*? People are not just what they do; they have a life under the surface, a world of private thoughts. And deep below this there is another self into which the residue of experiences is slowly sifting and the consequences for the future being determined. A girl is altered by these experiences, far more profoundly than she knows. They do not just begin and end, and leave no trace. We are responsible for each other's future. We are none of us just what we seem to be at the moment. It is so easy, if you happen to want the fun of going to bed with yet another girl, to accept her at her own temporary valuation so that you can get on with what you want. She will almost certainly have some doubts about what she is doing, a sort of restlessness, an occasional hope that somewhere real

companionship will be discoverable and something permanent achieved. So you have to do more than give your
neighbour the moderate love you give yourself, to give her
the same half-respect you have for yourself. You are neither
of you responsible only for the her-and-you situation; because you are both *human* you are responsible for your part
in the whole of creation. Your moment of love together is
not just an isolated moment in time; it is linked to everything else that happens and inevitably to the future.

You don't need to be confessedly religious to understand
this. You can reach it in your thought and you can feel it
in your bones if you will give yourself a chance. But a
Christian would want to say, as I am saying now, that the
commandment to love your neighbour as yourself is not
complete without the preceding one. *Thou shalt love the Lord
thy God with all thy heart.* If there is some glimmer of understanding of what this means, and an acceptance of it, then
loving another person takes you beyond the moment of
sensation to a realization of its place in the whole scheme
of things and to a satisfaction that has an eternal quality
in it.

Early in this chapter I showed that the conventional
moral code was in many respects superficial and certainly
an inadequate guide to your conduct. That was why I em-
barked on a search for a deeper, truer morality. Now we
ought to reconsider the moral code, to find just how much
use we really have for it. It would be too simple to say that
now that we have discovered a deeper morality to guide us,
we need think no longer about the moral code.

Some people have in fact taken this line, but the result
has hardly ever been what they hoped. People have, for
instance, decided to live together without getting married
– for various reasons. Some have said: 'Why bother about
the conventions? It doesn't make any real difference. Why
should we tie each other up by a legal agreement? So long
as we love each other we shall remain together. If we cease
to love each other ... well, to accept the appearance of
being married when we don't love each other is dishonest.'

Others have lived together unmarried because one partner could not dissolve a previous marriage. I think it would be true to say that all the people who have acted in this way have found their friendships, their community relationships, upset – unless they belonged to an easy-going group in which it was the 'done thing' to go against convention. But these easy-going groups are hardly ever communities in the sense of being groups of people who have depth, sincerity, tenderness, and reliability; they are not fully responsible groups of people. All too often they consist of discontented, rootless folk who fritter away their energies in a series of impermanent relationships. Those who have belonged to ordinary communities have had to meet serious difficulties – harsh judgements, misunderstanding, and embarrassment. Probably the most unhappy result is the effect on the children of such partnerships. They are, of course, illegitimate. I have known and taught many illegitimate children. In a welcoming and loving school community where boys and girls are accepted and valued as persons no matter what their colour, social class or origins, the fact of illegitimacy is irrelevant and quickly forgotten. Many illegitimate children do not get this help; so I can say emphatically that the most saddening aspect of irresponsible intercourse is that very many illegitimate children are born as a result and have to pay for their parents' heedlessness in suffering.

The unconventional couple might decide to have no children. But this is an injury to their relationship; it denies to the woman something that should be part of her love. It is a really terrible denial, and it puts into the relationship something that in the end may destroy the whole of love.

Another 'immoral' action in which young people are often involved is the decision to live together before getting married. These may be indeed people who genuinely love each other and are fully committed in mind and spirit. Many good marriages among one's friends have started in this way, and it might seem difficult to criticize this practice on either practical or fundamental grounds. Nevertheless, we have to try to look at it not only from the point of view of the particular relationship but also from the point of view of its effect upon people in the mass. We are all of us in some measure part of our community. As persons we inevitably depend on the community. In fact, as I said at the end of the chapter on *Persons*, we cannot have personality at all without being related in friendship and some sort of community life to other people. The community helps us to be what we are, and in turn all that we do affects the community. We may, in an assertion of independence, decide to behave as though there were no connexion with the community, but this can never in fact be true. It will work in this way. There are certain to be many who want to do as they please, no matter what the more responsible people may think or do. To some extent they are restrained by the moral code, and if that code seems to be weakening they will take advantage of it. A girl may know that a friend of hers is going to bed with the man she is engaged to, and is enjoying it. She will not know enough of the intimate side of the friendship to judge how deeply the pair are committed in mind, but she can't help knowing that they are 'having a good time'. How will this affect her when, after an exciting evening and a drink, her boy friend, who may have no responsible intentions at all, suggests a night together? This is not an imaginary situation; it is the sort of thing that happens very frequently where young people are living in close contact with each other. Young people *are* held back from acting foolishly by the awareness that there *is* a moral code; if they find that the people they respect are ignoring it, there is then nothing left to save them.

I'm not trying to produce arguments to convince you that in spite of all that I have said about the need for a truer morality, you *must* observe the conventional moral code. What, then, am I saying? First, that the moral code has a very important function. It implies that there must be some sort of standard; you need to have something to look at, think about, be challenged by, when you contemplate doing just what you want. There must be some sort of general safeguard, however imperfect, that protects people from their own wayward impulses and the demands of others. Morals are a sort of assertion by society as a whole that it cannot have chaos. Better any sort of order, any discipline, than none at all. Our morality has a historical foundation, it has been found *necessary*. Secondly, I would say that those who decide to break through the moral code must do so responsibly, knowing what they are doing, why they are doing it, and with some foresight as to the results. There is never any justification for breaking through the moral code just because you don't like it or because you have a convenient contempt for convention.

Moral codes do change with the passing of time. I do not know what the sexual morality of several hundred years hence will be; but I am pretty certain that it will differ in some respects from what it is now. It will be altered simply because people will behave differently. Whether the change will be to a better morality or a worse will depend upon whether people just smash convention or begin to behave with such sensitiveness and responsibility that a very restrictive moral code will not be necessary.

10

UNDERSTANDING GIRLS

WHAT are girls like? Very like you and very different from you. I think it is important to stress the way they are like you, because there is a strong tendency in all those things I have so often mentioned – books, papers, films, and so on – to represent girls as almost a different species, specially exciting because so extremely different and mysterious. This persists in spite of the fact that in the last fifty years women have come out of the drawing-room and the kitchen to work alongside men, to manage businesses, to handle machinery, and drive cars, to put on exceedingly unbecoming uniforms as railway porters or tube train attendants, even to be killed alongside men and drowned with them in war. Still the romantic vision persists, in spite of the fact that about one in six of the advertisements on the tube elevators reminds us that women are made of very ordinary flesh which supposedly has to be held in place by artificial means. Even he who thinks himself completely free from illusions may get a shock of surprise when he sees the massive buttocks and sturdy legs of a girl scrambling above him on a mountain-side.

Let us recognize, then, that girls have vigorous bodies that, in spite of the elaborate and delicate attentions given them, need no coddling. They are not capable of the great burst of energy and muscular effort that men can put out in a race, but they are capable of great endurance and can outlast men in conditions of privation and strain. But to say that a man can do the 100 metres in 10.1 seconds, whereas a woman does it in 11.3 seconds, and that a woman will last out a few hours or a few days longer than a man, is not to say that they are different, but that they are very alike, built to live and work and play together.

The most careful testing has not revealed any difference

in intelligence, or whatever it may be that is measured by intelligence tests. Girls and women may use their minds in different ways, but the fundamental abilities are equal to those of men. Boys who are at school with girls will observe certain differences of interests. For instance, girls become appreciative of poetry perhaps two years before boys have any use for it; that is because they become conscious of their own feelings and of the importance of the feeling side of life before boys do. You might think that there are many other differences that can be observed in school. But I have found that most of these are produced by the influence of the school or parents and are not due to the nature of girls. If you give girls the chance to do carpentry many will enjoy it and carry it on right through their school life – up to the age of 18! And they can be as good as boys. Some of them – not so many – do well in metal-work. If both boys and girls are taught to darn their socks, the boys will often do a neater job. Boys can become very good cooks.

There's one difference, noticeable at school and also throughout life. Boys are more inventive, more likely to try experiments and unusual things. This is to be seen in science classes, especially during practical work. A girl will tend to follow the instructions, work hard, get the job done efficiently, and her notes beautifully written up. A boy will dawdle, ask questions about something only remotely connected with the job, and try something other than what he has been told to do. Sometimes this will be sheer foolery, but sometimes it will be well worth while, giving him a feeling of having found out something for himself. I think it is true that on the whole men are more enterprising and daring in their thoughts and activities, women more conservative, steady, and thorough.

How does this tie up with behaviour? It is a well-known fact that there are far more criminal and maladjusted boys than girls of the same sort; I think there are fifteen times as many 'bad' boys as 'bad' girls. So you see the enterprise and initiative of boys is both a virtue and a fault; it can take them into crime as well as into genius. We say that there is more 'scatter' with boys than with girls. Boys are spread out, so to speak, all the way from the very bad to the genius; girls are more bunched up, not so many bad ones at the bottom end, not so many unusual ones at the top. But again I want to say that between the ordinary girl and the ordinary boy there is not a very great difference; they are indeed very much alike; and I think that it is important to start from this thought. If you accept this you will treat girls as having much in common with yourself, but enough differences to make friendship exciting and interesting. It is false and unfair to treat girls as dolls unable to understand 'a man's world'. There *are* fluffy-headed girls, but many of them have been made so because their men-folk encouraged it and did not encourage the intelligent and practical side. No, girls – certainly when they have grown up into mature women – have a great capacity to be steady, reliable, practical, and good organizers. I usually see a marked development in this direction between fifteen and eighteen.

Well then, if you have serious ideas that you discuss with other boys, share them with your girl friends too. Pay them the compliment of expecting them to understand. Worthwhile girls will appreciate this. You will discover differences of interest, but that is all to the good; it will help the development of your mind if you try to enter into their interests, and the corresponding thing will be good for them. Suppose you are beginning to be interested in politics. You will probably find that your girl friend is not interested. She will perhaps show a distaste for politics; this will most likely arise from her feeling that personal relationships in politics are bad and that the things that deeply matter in personal life are ignored or damaged by politics. It will be good for you to understand her feeling, because in fact politics and politicians easily go bad precisely because they ignore these things. On the other hand the girl must venture further than her feelings; she must realize that if we don't make political choices, intelligent choices, everything will suffer, including personal life. You will find that where women work together in large masses without much contact with men except after hours, their political ignorance, apathy, and childishness are appalling. On the other hand I must point out the cruelty and insensitiveness of men when they are herded together away from women. The best qualities of both men and women come to the surface when they work together, and it is then that they come nearest to the truth about life.

If after a fair trial your girl friend continues to be impatient with your attempts to share your serious thoughts and wants to be treated only as a doll that squeaks when it is squeezed, hadn't you better find someone else? She doesn't really want *you*.

I must say something more about the development of girls and the different sorts of girls. There are girls who from a very early age behave like dolls. I can't help calling them 'horrid little girls' although I know it is not their fault but the fault of their upbringing. These cultivate arch manners, use their eyes provocatively and seductively, wiggle their bodies, and generally draw attention to themselves. They want to be the centre of attention, they are acutely conscious of themselves; they are not conscious of you except to think of you as one who will pay attention to them.

Another girl of the same age, perhaps fourteen or fifteen, will be a bit of a tomboy, living most of the time in shorts or jeans, with her hair rarely combed and for ever wanting to crash in on the activities of boys, not to get attention from the boys, but because she wants to do the things they do. Many very wholesome and worth-while girls are like this. They envy, not without reason, the freedom that boys enjoy and they want to share it.

It is important to understand what is happening in such a girl, and also very important not to take advantage of it. Sometimes the boys, especially if some of them are a bit older and more sophisticated, begin to 'use' her physically, not necessarily in a specifically sexual way, but in the way of 'treating her rough', squeezing her violently, pushing her about, smacking her bottom. This is not a good thing to do. A girl in that stage must not be made conscious of her body as an object of attraction or excitement; the excitement *is* sexual even if the treatment is rough, and the effect on the girl is sexual. She ought to be allowed to be a 'good pal', to share the physical adventures as far as she can, and the fact that she is a girl should as far as possible be ignored. She's generally a more worth-while person than the simpering sort of the same age; treat her properly and she will make a fine companion and mate later. If she is allowed to grow up in her own way and at her own rate she will later begin to dress nicely, take care of her appearance, and look attractive, but she will probably retain her wholesome outward-looking attitude to life.

Throughout the teens there's one characteristic about girls you will notice – their preoccupation with personal matters. When boys are still playing with dinkie toys and conkers, girls are very much concerned with people. The interest can be very trivial, and usually is at this stage, though when urgently stirred about something the interest can go deep even in a twelve-year-old. At any stage in a girl's or a woman's life this interest in people and personal things can have a trivial or a serious expression, it can be silly, even damaging, or it can be deeply understanding and supremely valuable. You could put the interest on a sort of scale; at the bad extreme you could put gossip, tale-bearing, mischief-making, minding other people's business, being possessive and selfish about friends; at the other end – the good end – the most genuine concern for other people's happiness and health, readiness for complete self-sacrifice, great generosity and an ability to see right through all sorts of quibbles and excuses to the real heart of a personal problem.

When they become thoughtful, girls are extremely responsive. It matters to them tremendously how they are thought of, how they stand in other people's esteem. A girl will sink into utter misery if she has the slightest reason to think that you have no use for her; but a girl of only moderate talents or appearance will flower exuberantly if she discovers that you care about her and believe in her. Have you ever noticed how a girl, previously thought to be plain, can suddenly become radiant and seem quite a different person? I think this explains the very great variation in women, and is the reason why statements about women and the books written about them are so full of contradictions. To a far greater extent than boys and men, they vary according to what is thought of them and expected of them.

Now this places a big responsibility upon the boy or the man. If you have a poor opinion of girls, you will give them a poor opinion of themselves and they will begin to behave in a way that seems to prove that you were right. (This is only a very general statement; some have an innate strength that makes them more independent.) If the sort of girl you want is a silly giggling creature, you will find yourself surrounded by silly giggling creatures. If men spread around the idea that virginity doesn't matter and that girls ought to be good-time girls and go to bed with a man now and then, then they will tend to swing the girls in their social group in that direction. Girls reading this may be furious with me for saying it, but too many examples of it have come to my notice, and I shall have something to say about this later. I hope they will remember what I said above and realize that what is their weakness is also their strength; if something better is expected of them they can rise to greater heights in some respects than men. Moreover, if girls realize what they are like and do not merely repudiate the thought, they can make themselves more independent and refuse to respond to the degrading stimulus.

Now, there's a danger. Does it tempt you to say to yourself: 'Aha! What power I have! I can make what I like of girls; I can ennoble them, I can degrade them.' If you think this you will succeed only in degrading them, for to think of yourself as having *power* over them will be to make them only the instruments of power, just as dictators tend to turn men into strutting morons. If you set out to make a girl into something, even if that something is good or 'ideal', you will tend to make her into a type or a pattern, not a person – that is, if she doesn't guess what you are up to and run away. If a girl is to become wholly your partner, one who will delight and satisfy you permanently, she must respond to your essential *humanity*. This response can come only through humility on your part – for you are not better or worse than she is – and through a sincere, honest relationship in which you dispense with the wolf-whistle, the sophisticated patter of the man who knows all the ropes, the he-man stuff and the flirting, and allow her to know you as you really are.

I think a word is required here about girls and their clothes. They seem so tremendously important – and by clothes I mean what's underneath and on top and the hair-do and the make-up. I have mentioned often enough already the advertisements for the countless things that minister to a girl's interest in her own appearance. The magazines and the advertisements give us the impression that a girl or a woman is preoccupied with her own appearance to the exclusion of almost everything else. It is true that she is more interested in looking at herself in a mirror than ever members of the male sex are. It is apt to be a weakness and when exaggerated by a mistaken upbringing produces the self-absorbed type of girl that I have already mentioned. But it has to be remembered that the over-whelming impression we get of the importance of feminine attire and fripperies is due more to the intense competition of business interests than to the nature of women. Obviously very large profits are to be made by persuading women that a slight change in the shape of a bra or a girdle is necessary in order to keep abreast of fashion, and there must be a large section of the female population open to this sort of persuasion. But my impression is that most girls can laugh at it all, even if they indulge themselves for a while. Perhaps their boy friends can help them with a little laughter too, and an elementary exposition of the working of the capitalist system.

There's another thing that puzzles the more thoughtful boy sometimes. This is the curious contradiction that seems to exist in girls in the matter of modesty. Almost habitually he thinks of girls as being more modest than he, careful to arrange their skirts when sitting down and ready to scream if someone opens that bathroom door they've forgotten to lock. On the other hand he can't help noticing the evening-dress in which all the back and a considerable part of the breasts are exposed, and being aware of the way, in the entertainment world, it is accepted that women should expose as much of their bodies as the regulations will permit. He sees bathing costumes steadily diminishing in area and his sister and his girl friend taking every advantage of the opportunity. In generations past there was a sharp distinction between 'decent women', whom Bernard Shaw once described as not clothed but upholstered, and the Gaiety Girl who wore as little as possible. Now they *all* wear as little as possible, on the appropriate occasion. The boy knows that his sister and his girl friend are not 'fast' and that they would be horrified if the exposure of their bodies was thought of as naughty.

The fact of the matter is that the modesty of girls is not real. In their nature they are definitely less modest than boys. I've mentioned that there are many families today in which there is no training in artificial modesty; the children are not always told that they must cover themselves and lock the bathroom door. It is noticeable that if any of the youngsters in such a family develop a natural modesty it will be the boys rather than the girls. The girls are more likely than the boys not to bother about the bathroom door. Very conventional people reading this may be horrified and consider that such girls are far from nice. This is quite mistaken. The girls are completely innocent; it simply does not occur to them that there is anything shameful about their nakedness. A boy on the other hand becomes acutely conscious of his sexuality in his teens. His sex organs constantly remind him of it, and nakedness tends for him to become a distinctly sexual experience. This is disturbing to many boys and drives them towards privacy. A girl, however, tends to take her body as part of her personality. She may sometimes be a little troubled by her menstrual periods if they are painful, but in general she accepts her body happily and enjoys it. She is sensuous in her enjoyment of it and usually has no reason to feel that there is anything wrong about this. She likes to feel her body caressed by the clothes she wears, hence the frequent experimenting with new materials, and the glamorous tights. She likes the feel of them against her skin, and so delighted is she with the texture given to the surface of her skin by an expensive pair of stockings that she will wear them even when she risks laddering them first time.

A boy who allowed himself to have all these feelings about his body would have a bad conscience, or would think of himself as distinctly different from other boys. The only sort of experience the average boy allows himself to enjoy is the glow he feels after a swim, the wind blowing through his shirt, or the sun beating on his skin.

Now all this makes girls dangerous. They *are* dangerous, the best of them! So often they have no idea of what they are doing to men and boys, precisely because they are innocent of any conscious intentions and no one has told them how easily a boy is sexually aroused. Some of the most natural and unsophisticated girls can find themselves in awkward situations because men have mistaken their innocence for a come-hither signal. So girls have to be *taught* modesty. Usually, however, this is done without the other part of the training – the teaching about the sexuality of men. Girls ought to know about this too before they are launched on the world. But it has to be carefully done, otherwise it may have the wrong effect, the effect of making the girl aware of her power to stimulate men and of tempting her to use it. The teaching has to be backed up by a real sense of responsibility. It takes only a little of the wrong sort of excitement to turn an innocent girl into one who deliberately exposes bits of herself and is found in bathroom situations that are not accidental.

Here comes a difficult point. It is very necessary for young men to discriminate between the girl who is innocently free in her behaviour and the girl who is playing tricks. The fact that a girl hasn't much concern for physical modesty must not be taken as showing that she is a fast type or is inviting your attentions. When men try to take advantage of situations involving a girl of this sort they are often rebuffed, and then they exclaim 'Well, you asked for it!' She may have done nothing of the kind. Men who behave and talk in this way are simply acting according to the 'rules of the game' instead of trying to know and understand people. Now for the difficulty. I have used the phrase 'innocent of intentions' in the previous paragraph. But any experienced person watching girls will notice behaviour that is innocent of intentions yet is definitely provoking. Something quite unconscious in the girl is driving her to create a sexual situation. Nature intends girls for motherhood and reproduction and provides them with impulses that drive them towards these experiences. These impulses make girls behave in such a way as to invite the male. You don't need to wait for the teens to observe this; you can see it in a girl of five who cannot possibly know what she is doing.

So now we have a possible complication in the girl who does not bother much about modesty and may innocently enjoy a scanty bathing suit. Nature may in fact be hard at work in her, pushing her towards the inevitable end; but she doesn't know it. Nature may be equally hard at work in the girl who makes a great fuss about modesty and who, at the seaside, makes an elaborate performance of finding a rock large enough to change behind. She is drawing intense attention to her body; but she doesn't know it. Does this weaken the caution I have given you about taking advantage of what you think is a come-hither signal? Does it mean that you can say that her behaviour *is* after all a request that you should touch her, and one that you should respond to?

The answer is a very big NO! A very large part of human behaviour comes from unconscious impulses. If we allowed ourselves always to respond in a primitive way to the primitive impulses that we inferred in other people's behaviour we should all be murdering each other long before we had any time for sex. Nearly all young women behave in an unconsciously sexual way in the presence of an eligible man, and nearly all men alter their behaviour to a more sexual pattern when a charming girl comes into the room. How dull life would be if they didn't! But normal girls are much more unaware than men are of what they are doing sexually and it should be a matter of chivalry, or if that has no appeal nowadays, of good-sportsmanship, not to take advantage of the fact. What you should always do is to wait, proceed gently and patiently until there are unmistakable signs that you are wanted, until *conscious* desires emerge on which you can proceed confidently and responsibly. We are human beings, not just animals.

It is good to swing back and forth between the personal and the sexual in one's thoughts about girls; so now I turn again to some problems that are found in the more general interchanges between boys and girls. I greatly enjoy having boys and girls together when serious matters are being discussed. It must be dull, dealing only with boys or only with girls! Although they may be equally intelligent, they often make characteristically different contributions to a discussion. Boys can become immensely excited over an argument in itself, without caring very much whether it is closely connected with the practical point from which it started. It does not matter to them whether the argument has any practical importance; it can be right up in the air and they can enjoy it without feeling that it is necessary to bring it down to earth. Girls tend to be impatient with this tendency; they are much more 'down to earth' and when the discussion shows signs of wandering away from the practical issue they want to call it back. Now this difference is a valuable one. Out of the airy speculations of the male mind some valuable theory has been spun, which has eventually proved of practical value, for instance in science. But there are times when this speculation is obviously sterile, producing nothing. It is necessary that men should be made aware when they are just blowing themselves up with their own hot air. In an argument, women can often make them aware of this, though they run a serious risk of having their criticism impatiently rejected! Male pride is involved.

On the other hand, women can be too much down to earth; their discussion of a problem can be too pedestrian, not enough enlivened by imaginative speculation. What should be clear, then, is that when men and women accept and understand their differences, and when they are willing to work patiently together, we often have the best possible conditions. Each stimulates, challenges, and corrects the other.

There is a further point to be recognized: no one is completely male or completely female. That is even true about the body, but it is even more true about personality. There are two consequences that should be noted. One is that what I have said about the differences between men and women, between boys and girls will not always be as clear as I have suggested. Some boys will show a tendency to think and feel as girls do, while some girls will show a distinctly masculine streak which will moderate their femininity. I have described the extremes, and real people whom you know should not be expected to conform exactly to type. The second consequence is that we should not neglect the feminine in ourselves. If men and boys do neglect this or squash it, they become insensitive and often brutal. There has been something of a tradition that boys and men should not express deep and tender feelings in their everyday life, that to do so would be 'sissy'. This is what has been called 'the taboo on tenderness' and it is most unfortunate; it may explain many of the evils that men are responsible for in the world. A man in whom the latent, or hidden, feminine side is not developed will too readily tolerate cruelty and be unaware of the many subtleties in life which we must know if we are to act wisely. On the other hand, when women neglect the masculine in themselves they tend to become just mirrors, the mirrors of what men want. But when both sexes are together, each trying honestly and patiently to understand the other, a full development in each is likely to take place – a development of both sides of the personality.

Not only do boys and girls tend to approach a problem in a different way, but they are aware of different *facts*. They notice different things, different aspects of a situation. I find this specially so when boys and girls in responsible positions discuss a school problem; the boys often have a very good grasp of the whole situation and its relation to past and future procedure, whereas the girls know much more clearly what are the personal issues under the surface, who is in trouble or who is likely to be involved in difficulties if a certain action is taken. If we are to act wisely in any situation we need to know all the facts involved. A great deal of time is given in schools to the training of children to think clearly, but not enough time is given to helping children to become wide-awake to things that really matter in their lives. What is the use of being able to think clearly if you don't notice the things that ought to be thought about? Men and women tend to notice different things as they go about the world, and if they work together and pool their information, they will all know more about life and will be able therefore to think and act more effectively.

Now for an awkward fact that will certainly appear in attempts on the part of boys and girls to understand each other. It is important to know what it means to be 'objective'. It means to see things as nearly as possible as they really are. If you have something wrong with your eyes – colour-blindness or a distorted lens – your view of an object will be upset. It will be 'subjective', made false by the condition of your – the subject's – eyes. All our awareness of the world around us is to some extent made false by our habits and prejudices, resulting from the way we have been brought up and the experiences we have been through. Our *desires* have a very strong effect in making us tend to see things wrongly. Scientists expecially have to correct each other time and time again to make sure that they are not following a bad habit or claiming false results because they are the results they would *like* to have. There is a familiar saying that 'the wish is father to the thought'. If you *want* a thing to be so, you will be strongly inclined to produce wonderful arguments to prove that it *is* so. If we put aside politicians and other men who are involved in emotional situations and who get heated, we can say that on the whole men find it easier to be objective than women. They can often to a large extent put aside their own feelings and consider a matter dispassionately. They can get themselves out of the picture.

A girl's difficulty in doing this is connected with her deep interest in personal things and the way she tends to take things deep into her feelings. How often I have tried to cope with some crazy situation in which a girl has been involved and have told her the truth about it in the simplest, clearest logical terms! It makes no impression whatever. All she can say is: 'Yes I know, *but* ...!' The logic has no impact on the feelings, and I have just to wait till later. Similarly a girl has the greatest difficulty in seeing herself from another's point of view. Often she can't be objective about herself except by seeing herself through the eyes of a man she loves. If a man she doesn't care for tries to tell her about her faults a difficult situation is apt to arise. One of the things that teachers in co-educational schools have to learn is that they must never use sarcasm to discipline their pupils. A boy can throw it off; when the master's back is turned he puts his thumb to his nose. But it goes right down into the soul of a girl; she feels attacked as a *person*, and she is likely to repudiate that teacher for ever.

Men sometimes try to convince women of what they think to be truth by hammering away at them with closely reasoned logical arguments, and the more the women push them away, the harder they argue, so that exasperation is the final result. One of the most intelligent men I have ever known, a brilliant scholar and administrator, a master of many languages and a man for whom mathematics was his bedtime reading, and indeed a very lovable man, completely failed to make a common life with his wife because he could not understand that her mind did not work as his did.

I must be careful to say that there are variations between one woman and another, between one girl and another. Some are more objective, some less. And what I have said must not be taken to mean that women cannot be good scientists or research workers in other fields. Scientific work exerts such a rigorous, almost automatic discipline that women who take it up become as objective – within that part of their life – as men.

It looks as if this is a real weakness in women. But we all, men and women, boys and girls, have the weaknesses that go with our strengths and our virtues. If women take things deeper down into themselves and get more easily hurt, it is also true that their response in a situation of need often comes from deeper down. They often know much more truly than men do what is the real need in a human situation, and their response is more generous.

11

MAKING FRIENDS WITH THEM

IN this chapter I am going to think in a more detailed fashion about the behaviour of boys and girls together, keeping in mind the main principles that I have already suggested. I should remind you briefly of what these principles are. One is that friendship should be the basis of any sex relationship, and that this friendship is the same as any true friendship between two people of the same or opposite sexes anywhere. Another is that friendship and love must be based on a true appreciation and respect for the other person as an independent human being, quite apart from anything that you may hope to get from the other person. Yet another is the need for a generous valuation of the mind and feelings of the person you love, the acceptance of equality with a recognition of differences.

It will be something of a jump backwards to turn from these principles to a consideration of the way boys under thirteen behave! Perhaps the most obvious thing about boys of this age is the way they go around in a gang. They haven't much use for girls outwardly. If they are in a mixed class and can sit where they like, it is very noticeable how they tend to keep in a bunch away from the girls. In many of their activities outside school they ignore girls. They don't invite the girls to join in their play. Their contacts with girls are often teasing relationships, involving petty annoyances and even jeering, which may be harmless but which sometimes becomes unpleasant. Occasionally ragging takes place and a girl may be the victim. It is at this stage, and a little later, that the boys are most likely to be obsessed with dirty language and preoccupied with the anatomical aspect of sex and intercourse. This goes round and round among themselves but now and then a girl becomes the object of sexual suggestions and is upset and hurt by it. The boys have practically no idea of what is possible in friendship and affection between the sexes at this stage, but they are quick to observe what is happening between boys and girls a few years older. Frequently these affairs between older boys and girls become the object of jeering and unpleasant suggestion from the gang whose members tend to think only of what the couples might be doing sexually, not having the experience or the imagination to understand what might be going on in the way of real friendship. Thus it is difficult for the boy and girl of, say, sixteen, to conduct a friendship without having the purely sexual possibilities thrust under their noses. The thirteen-year-olds need frequently to be checked, told what is the effect of what they are doing, and helped to see that they are spoiling the freedom of relationship that the older ones ought to have – a freedom that they themselves will want to have in their turn.

The behaviour of a gang of this sort is an example of sex hostility. It would be good to be able to say that this hostility vanishes with increase in age, but it does not necessarily. Love and hate seem always to be very close together. It is what is called *ambivalence*, feeling-both-ways. I have already shown how, when love breaks down in a sexual relationship, the quarrelling that follows is often more bitter than a quarrel between members of the same sex. This is a basic human tendency; by understanding it we can get on top of it, but it is certainly there in us. Not only is there evidence of sex hostility in the intimate life of people who seem in other respects to love each other, but there is evidence of it in the mass-behaviour of people. Men who show their wives plenty of affection when they are at home are sometimes guilty of the most cynical and hostile remarks about 'women' if they have to meet a woman who is in authority over them or if a woman invades some clubroom or other place sacred to men. The bitter struggle that women had to go through in order to get the vote showed how deeply hostile men in the mass could be to women, and how both 'love' and contempt can exist together in one person. This may seem a very difficult idea to get hold of. But it may become a bit clearer if we think further about the way boys in a gang behave.

These gangs exist at all ages and in all levels of society, though it is noticeable that when boys and girls live to-gether in a community – it might be a school or a village – where the adults are in close contact with children and standards are generally good, the gang impulse weakens very much towards sixteen and a general mixing takes place. But often one sees the gang going on well into adult-hood; and where there are gangs there is sex hostility. Watch a gang at the street corner. Two or three girls pass, arm-in-arm. There are whistles and suggestive remarks. The girls pass on. The boys turn to each other and exchange grins, knowing looks, intimate remarks. The implication seems to be that the boys are a closely-knit group with certain ideas and attitudes in common. They are intimately held together by a common attitude towards girls. They are a bit like a group of hunters, watching their prey, ready to pounce. When one of them 'gets a girl' it is not with the intention of making a relationship with her that is intimate and understanding in the same way as his relationship with the gang is intimate. It is a wholly different thing. It is something that he can report back to the group about – report back to the other chaps who also understand the game. For a brief period just after the First World War I did some holiday work on ration cards, in an office crowded with recently demobilized soldiers. Almost the whole of their talk was of this character, about the girl a man got last night, and what he did with her, and so on. It was the *men* who understood each other; there was never a sugges-tion that a man and a woman might understand each other.

In much more cultured circles there is still a tendency for men to congregate and, without necessarily any coarse talk, to produce an atmosphere like adventurers coming back to where they belong after their travels. Sex is an excursion – a temporary one – into foreign territory. Even among married men there is often a loyalty to the other men which is in some ways stronger than the loyalty to wife and home. Among his pals a man's wife becomes 'the wife'.

What divided creatures human beings are! They want peace but they make war. They love to build cars and ships and homes and cathedrals, but they also enjoy destruction, to see a bomb destroy a house or sink a ship, just as a child loves to see his tower of bricks collapse as he pulls away the bottom brick. And people are divided about sex; they want it to be lovely but they seem impelled to make it messy. A boy wants a girl to be his most intimate friend and yet he talks to his pals as though girls were their prey.

How can you get over this division in yourself? Generally speaking, by stopping talking and dreaming and by making something different of your group-life. These gangs spend so much time talking about girls instead of getting to know them. Girls don't get together in gangs in quite the same way as boys do, but they do spend an awful lot of time gossiping. As one young woman reported to me, 'It's very queer, but more than half a girl's love-life is spent discussing her affair with other girls!' The effect of this gang-life and these gossip groups is to get the whole matter out of perspective; they make the purely sexual and the romantic side far too immediately important, they make it difficult for a boy and girl to meet as human beings. One of the obvious effects of the gang-life on a boy's or a young man's attitude is that as soon as he meets an attractive girl he begins to undress her with his eyes or to wonder what she would be like to go to bed with. Sex gets in the way of their knowing each other.

I have said that you should *do* something instead. Get the groups to mingle, encourage activities in which boys and girls get together and which haven't anything specially to do with sex: hobbies, discussions, sports, and strenuous journeys, dramatics, practical work of every sort. Find opportunities to meet girls in evening classes, in political or community service groups, in acting, sailing or climbing clubs – anything where both sexes are interested in something that doesn't all the time remind them of sex. This won't stop sex, but it will give an opportunity for the other needs in a friendship to come into mind, to be recognized and fulfilled. When there is discussion about boy-and-girl problems, see that both sexes are present. Try to get a serious attitude so that even intimate problems of sex can be wholesomely discussed in a mixed group. It's when girls or boys go off into a huddle that the balance and perspective are lost.

Young people are often reluctant to look ahead at the request of someone much older, even though their own dreams are very much occupied with the future. But can you get some picture in your mind of what sort of adult life you want to live? When you look around at the adult world, don't you find that the soundest community, the social group in which there is a continuous enjoyment of life, is one in which men and women work together freely without falsely worked up excitement? Sex doesn't die under these conditions; indeed these are the conditions under which sex is most satisfying. Remember that all the time I am concerned that men and women should *enjoy* each other, very deeply and fully, and that their enjoyment should not be spoilt by mixed feelings or guilt or the memory of injuries done to each other.

During the difficult period of the teens, you should try to get a varied experience of friendship with girls. That implies that you should not make such a close friendship with one girl that you shut out others. Falling in love and getting married should be a *choice*, not a helpless falling into a gulf. To make a choice you must *know* something. That is as true of choosing a partner as it is of choosing a career. There is too much emphasis on getting and having a girl; the emphasis should be more on knowing girls. Of course what I have said does not mean, when the time comes to get engaged, that you will sit down and make a list of all the possible girls with their faults and virtues attached. No, you will be drawn to a certain girl because in the whole pattern of her personality she will have qualities that you will have learnt to recognize and value in your wider experience of people. Your mind will be working *with* your feelings.

There is a difficulty you will have to face, caused by the nature of girls. Girls are generally more possessive, more 'sticky' about their friendships than boys are. This is true of them among themselves. A girl wants to have a close personal friend and when she has got her she tends to hold on to her jealously and tightly. There's an awful lot of fuss about the making and breaking of these friendships. This happens too in a girl's friendship with a boy. So a girl will hold on to her boy friend more closely than he will hold on to her, and it will make it difficult for the boy to walk and talk with other girls. But girls must learn to be less possessive, just as boys must learn to be less casual, and they can learn these lessons from each other.

There are certain social customs that make worse difficulties, or that make the inevitable difficulties much worse than they need be. The one that immediately comes to mind concerns dances. It is the now well-established habit of dancing with the same partner for practically the whole of the evening. The result is that a girl has to get a boy friend or run the risk of being almost wholly neglected. When she has secured one she has to be possessive about him. I have heard it said of college dances that girls who go without a partner may not get more than four or five dances in as many hours, and when they do get them they are apt to feel that they are being pitied. This situation makes girls desperate; it turns them into birds of prey, and men are almost openly hunted. It may be the chief reason why in this last generation girls have seemed more openly out to get a man. Dances matter a great deal to young people and something therefore must be done to break this wretched habit. There is far too much complacency about it, far too little recognition of the harm and the hurt that result. A first step can be taken by a group of people going to a dance pledged at least to vary their partners within the group as much as possible and deliberately setting out to include 'unattached' people of both sexes. Young men should feel an obligation to unattached girls, to see that they have dances, so that girls will be encouraged to come to dances without feeling that they must first stalk a man.

Because dances play such a large part in the leisure time of young people I think it is well worth while to give some thought to the question of what makes a dance a wholly enjoyable event for everyone, not a hectic experience punctuated with heart-burnings, jealousies, and the sight of people making an exhibition of themselves. Like every other activity, it requires some control, some accepted discipline, and a few people to take responsibility. I have been present at dances in co-educational schools for over twenty-five years, and in my own school we have established a tradition that boys change their partners after nearly every dance and do not neglect the shy girls. There is also an unwritten rule, which never has to be mentioned, that you should not take sexual advantage of the dance to hug and caress your partner or to hold her unnecessarily close. The dances are extremely vigorous and gay; there are no dull, lifeless faces, and they end with expressions of satisfaction and delight. I am proud of what we have achieved – but it has happened because we gave *thought* to it. We had to know what we wanted and what to avoid. Even in schools this standard is not always achieved and dances can degenerate into affairs run by a few for their own benefit and attended by others who hope to enjoy themselves but rarely do. In dances at big institutions where there is less community feeling the good standard will obviously be much harder to achieve, but it is worth working for.

Perhaps a good deal of trouble in the teens, especially sexual trouble, is due to young people not knowing what they want or not being encouraged to think about it. The wants that come to human beings casually, from moment to moment, conflict with each other. To try to satisfy each as it comes is to get into a mess. So it is necessary to sort them out and judge them. The teens ought to be a time of sorting-out, when you gradually get clearer in your mind what you want and need most. It is not only what you want by way of enjoyment or in your career, but also what *values* you will search for and what qualities you appreciate in people. I ought to give some examples of what I mean by values. To sort out your values is to sort out your experiences in order of their worth-whileness, asking yourself whether each gives only a transitory pleasure, whether it leaves a bad taste in the mouth, whether it leaves a permanent satisfaction and makes you feel richer in personality. Will it be more important to you to make money and have a large car or to have a family? Which interests you more, getting to the top yourself or getting justice for other people? In your career do you want to become eminent or will you forget that aim in the sheer interest of the job? Do you prefer the flashy to the sound? Is it more important for you to impress the neighbours than to be honest and sincere? Is pleasure so important to you that you are prepared to take it at someone else's expense? Do you tend to take as true 'what the other chaps say' or what you have always said, or are you prepared to search for truth by doubting your own opinions?

Asking these questions insistently of yourself will not only clear your own mind to some extent but also give you a better basis on which to judge other people and your future partner. But it is important to have humility in judging the various girls you know. They are growing as you are growing and they are just as unfinished. They too are growing up in a world that tends to warp and twist them and give them false values. Like you they swing backwards and forwards, sometimes backwards to childishness, sometimes forward to responsibility and maturity. But by the time you have finished the teens you ought to be able to discover whether you and your girl friend share the same values and can depend on them in each other. That is much more important in the long run than the fun you get out of caressing each other. That fun will not last more than a few months if you haven't the same fundamental values. After that you will find yourselves at odds about some serious question and suddenly the physical side will 'go dead' or you will be torn between love and hate. Sometimes people at this point are seized with a sort of rage when they find that sex has nothing to support it, and they vent that rage on their partner.

One of the difficulties that a boy may have to face is a strain between himself and his parents over sex matters. Most parents begin badly; they fail at the very beginning, when a child who is little more than a toddler asks his first questions about babies or about the difference between his own body and a girl's. They are embarrassed, they can't give a straight answer, and ever after the gulf between themselves and the child widens. During the boy's adolescence the parents become frightened, knowing how easy it is for young people to be driven by sexual impulses into painful and tragic situations. The teenage son, aware of their fear and mistrust, keeps his sexual interests hidden and his friendships with girls secret. He may even make these friendships furtive. If you get to this point, however mild and innocent the relationship may have been at first, you will find it increasingly difficult to bring your *judgement* to bear on it. Love-affairs are heated up and romanticized by secrecy. It would be better to say to yourself that you will try to do something to overcome your parents' embarrassment, from your side. It may require only an opening from you to make a new and deeper relationship with your parents possible. They were probably no different from you when they were young and it may be a happy experience for them to share their common humanity with you. If it makes it possible for your early love-affairs to be openly acknowledged, known to the family, that will be a great gain. Two people cannot know each other until they have seen each other against the ordinary background of everyday life and family. If you want to know what your girl friend is like you must be able to stand back and see her in her own family circle or among her own friends. You must see her joining in activities that do not concern you. You must see her enjoying other people, perhaps quarrelling with them. She must see you in similar circumstances.

A further and very important point is that if your friendship with a girl is out in the open and part of a family and community life you will both find it easier to control yourselves, easier to avoid the dangerous situations and actions which bring boy-and-girl affairs into discredit. As I have pointed out, a furtive affair is likely to become intense, guilty, and obsessive.

It is time we considered the problem of control in some detail. I wonder if I have made the need for it clear enough? Every single human impulse or ability needs a discipline – a discipline that you yourself accept and apply. If you are unwilling to learn the discipline of handling tools in a workshop you will destroy machinery and waste material; if you are unwilling to learn the discipline of cricket you will be able to spend little time at the wicket. And if you do not realize that there is a necessary discipline in friendship you will offend people right and left. This discipline that I speak of has nothing to do with the discipline that one person exerts over another, for instance in the army. It is the discipline you impose on yourself in order to do something well. It is acquired by watching yourself and learning, becoming more and more able to direct your energy so that you have fewer mistakes to regret. This is necessary in love as in every other activity.

Sex, however, is a far more powerful impulse than the impulse to do carpentry or play cricket. If let loose completely it would produce violence, misery, and chaos. I have already said something about the proper use of the long waiting period between the time when your sex organs become ready for use and the time when you can get married. The alternatives are these. You can say: 'It's a nuisance; why the hell should I put off sex experience until I can get married, why shouldn't I have some fun on the quiet?' Or you can say: 'This is going to hurt; it's going to be a struggle. But I can get to know myself in the process and understand better what I really want.' One of my chief reasons for writing this book is to assure you that you can go through this struggle without feeling in the least guilty about the impulses that you have to control. You will be to that extent happier than many boys of an older generation who were never told that.

I said that an undisciplined carpenter will destroy material. The tragic fact about undisciplined sex is that it damages, and sometimes almost completely destroys, *people*. There always has to be another person – a person for whom you cannot help being responsible as well as for yourself. You are still responsible for her even if she joins you entirely of her own free will, as she is also for you.

Many boy-and-girl affairs begin without much of a conscious sex impulse in them. The two are pleasantly excited by each other's company, but the attraction remains 'idealistic' and romantic rather than specially sexual. The kisses that are exchanged are brief and not deeply stirring, and they need not be connected with any thought of further sexual activities. Boys and girls can go in and out of several such affairs before a more definitely sexual desire arises. But the age at which this desire appears tends to become lower as time goes on. Girls menstruate and become sexually mature earlier than they used to a hundred years ago, and the profusion of sexual entertainment and suggestion puts ideas into boys' and girls' heads before they need be there. So the boy may soon be aware of the deeper sexual stirring that follows a kiss and may want a more intimate contact. This is the point at which a decision has to be made. It is possible that the girl will not be equally roused; kissing may satisfy an inexperienced girl for a long time, and it may be years before her sexual organs begin to respond – unless the boy deliberately deepens the physical intimacy. Sometimes girls can go in and out of several teenage affairs and never know what it is to be sexually roused until they are extensively caressed by a man. This is one of the facts that a boy should keep in mind. There may be no urgency in the girl to carry the physical intimacy any deeper, and the friendship can remain warm, personally intimate, and faithful, without this further intimacy happening. If the boy decides – or allows himself to be impelled

– to explore further, he may make the situation dangerous and create so much tension that the relationship will lose its quality as a friendship and become obsessively sexual. To avoid 'trouble' the only way may be to bring the whole relationship to an end. What do you want most – a faithful friendship which may later become a lasting sexual relationship, or a sexual affair which must end friendship because it has come too soon to be manageable?

Girls are adaptable, they are generous. They all too often take their cue from the boy. Some who have been wisely prepared by their parents may be able to take a full and equal responsibility for controlling the extent of caressing. Some, not so prepared, will hardly know what is coming until it happens and will be all too ready to do what you want. So the heavier responsibility may rest on you. Can you refrain from doing things that sexually rouse her? Are you willing to let her go on for a few more years without having her life complicated, and her development prejudiced by the urgencies and longings of sex? A girl can be roused at fourteen. But she is very far from being grown up in any other respect. She has a host of things to learn, many adjustments to make before she can properly face the adult world. Why should she have to cope with sexual longings that could have remained dormant for another two, three, or even four years? From what I know of student life I can say that it is a wonder that many of the women get through any examinations at all, so preoccupying are the personal and sexual problems that assault them between eighteen and twenty-one. The schoolgirl at least should be allowed to remain free from this. Remember that sex is much more concerned with the whole of a girl than it is with the whole of a boy. A boy can misbehave sexually yet carry on his ordinary job or study as though unaffected. A girl's whole life is likely to be disturbed.

Even in the boy there are serious difficulties that may arise, and the more so if the boy is in general thoughtful and sensitive. Extensive sexual caressing can be enthralling and obsessive and nearly always introduces complications into life which the personality is not sufficiently developed to cope with properly. It must be emphasized that sex is savage and powerful and may easily take charge of us. If two people go beyond a certain point in their love-making it may be impossible for them to stop, no matter how good and responsible they are in other respects. About half of the girls who get married before the age of twenty are already pregnant when they take that step, and presumably many of them get married in a hurry so that they will not feel disgraced by the birth of an illegitimate child. They – and the boys – are not necessarily *bad*. They simply got into a situation in which the primitive impulses took charge. A large proportion of these early marriages are failures; the people concerned were not the right partners for each other and if they had had more time they would have recognized this fact.

It is even more true of girls than it is of boys and young men that there comes a point in love-making where they no longer have any control over themselves and will let anything happen. As one girl said, referring to an occasion when she had got trapped in a sexual situation with a man for whom she had no affection whatever, 'You go down, down. You don't care about anything, not even whether you will have a baby. You don't care, you don't think; you only feel.'

A number of young people do indulge in extensive caressing – 'petting' – and manage to stop short of sexual intercourse. Often this leaves the body nervously strung up and it is sometimes followed by pains in the back and abdomen. If petting happens occasionally over a short period, as is often the case with engaged couples, it doesn't matter; but when young people, who have no intention or possibility of marriage, see each other frequently and allow this petting, the result can be disturbing. The mind cannot be detached from the body, and to put the body into a condition of frequent tension can easily upset the relation between the partners and perhaps their future attitude towards sex.

12

TO YOUNG MEN–
ESPECIALLY STUDENTS

THE last chapter brought me finally to the problems of the young man rather than those of the boy. There is of course no dividing line between boyhood and manhood, and no particular age at which men are suddenly driven towards the act of intercourse. Much of what I now have to say may come at the right moment for a boy of sixteen or for a man of twenty-two. I am going to deal with the circumstances in which a strong desire for intercourse arises, and with the considerations that may pass through a young man's mind as he decides to indulge or to refrain.

You may wonder why I am specially addressing myself to students. There are two reasons. I hear more about student life than about the life of young men engaged in industry. Further, everything that can happen between young people happens between students; so that if I talk to students I shall be fairly certain to cover the problems of other young people too. If you are not a student, think of yourself as listening in, sorting out from what I say the things that might apply to you and to the other young people among whom you move. Students are not superior beings. It is true that they have certain mental abilities which make them suitable for education in colleges and universities; but apart from that they are not very different from the rest of mankind. They are, for instance, no better able to manage their personal affairs than are other young people. The management of personal affairs, the conduct of friendship, the discipline of working together, the wise direction of a love-affair, require an ability different from 'brains', and the young man in an office or a mill may have the ability as strongly as a boy who gets a scholarship to Oxford or Cambridge.

You might think that a young man knocking about in

the world, meeting all the sorts of people to be found in industry or in travel, would be more exposed to unfortunate and evil influences than his opposite number in the cloistered world of the university. I doubt this. The ordinary boy who goes out to work often remains near his home, continues to be a member of his community, mixes with all ages, and finds his friends where he has always found them. The student, however, goes into a new world in which there are all types of men and women, in which the impulse to shock is deliberately fostered and admired, and where he mixes almost wholly with people of his own age. It's a hot-house where strange plants grow all too easily.

Let me suppose for the purpose of this chapter that you, the reader, are a student. Perhaps you have just arrived at the university from a grammar school. Unless the university is in your home town, you are away from your parents for the first time. There will no longer be anyone to ask you what you were doing last night when you were so late home. Or perhaps you have come from a boarding-school. If that is so, you will probably have a great sense of release. At school you were hedged about by rules and regulations, most of which were framed to keep fourteen-year-olds in order and were not really appropriate to eighteen-year-olds. Now you are away from all that, and from the anxious pressure and perhaps heavy moralizing of your teachers. Whatever school you have come from, you are right away now from the watchful eye. If you are at Oxford or Cambridge or living in a hostel you will still have to obey certain regulations and perhaps occasionally pay fines, but I doubt whether anyone will be deeply concerned about what particular nocturnal activity keeps you out after the gates are closed.

Isn't this an immense relief? Of course it is. But isn't it also rather a sudden change? What are you making of it?

It is normal that young men and women should be rebellious and should thumb their noses to authority. It can even be said to be desirable, for authority is apt to go bad if it is not challenged. But the rebelliousness is often artificially boosted by the senselessness of the restrictions from which they have just escaped; and if they have been made to show respect for authority merely because it is authority there will be a much greater impulse to show that they no longer have any respect for it or for the demands it supports. This explains in part the crazy things that students do – the rags that they could never have got away with at school, the drinking that was forbidden before, and sex. But isn't it a pity that sex should be mixed up in this? If sexual actions were done just because of sexual urges we should know more clearly where we were; but in fact much of the energy of young people's sexual activities derives from the fact that sex is being used as an instrument of rebellion, a form of defiance. In no other activity is the conflict between authority and the individual, between the old and the young, so intense. So what we see is not just sex expressing itself 'naturally', but sex exaggerated and distorted by the pattern of which it has become a part. It might be well for every student to ponder this. It *is* a distortion of sex to use it to defy authority. It puts sexual activity on a level with sexual swear words.

Students talk endlessly; and one of the things you will have to beware of is the tendency to believe that you can arrive at the truth about sex and life by much discussion. Argument can be intoxicating without help from alcohol; and it is easy to deceive yourself into thinking that you are being 'rational' when you use your intellect to analyse and debunk most of the ideas of the past – especially those ideas that seem to restrict your freedom to do exactly as you want. Beneath all the argument, the brilliance, and the wit, there remains the savage, making the logic serve his own instinctive purposes. A simple example of this is the frequently heard argument: *The sexual morality demanded of us is Christian. I am not a Christian; you are not a Christian. The morality therefore does not apply to us.* It is an argument that could be spread out over an hour or more's discussion.

HE AND SHE

There is a very strong urge in every one of us to reject the
morality so that we can misbehave ourselves with an easier
conscience! That should lead us to suspect the logic. Now
look at the statement. It is true only if you can in fact
choose to be a Christian or not to be, just as you might
choose to be or not to be a member of a political party.
But suppose that Christianity is not just an imposed dogma,
a club-membership belief; suppose that it contains the
truth about human life.* Then you can no more deny it
than you can deny gravitation. If this is a fact then the
only way left to you now is to attack conventional morality
on the grounds that it is not sufficiently or genuinely
Christian, or that the application of the truths of Christianity in these matters is a mistaken one.

I suggest that you distrust every intellectual argument
that is connected with your own or other people's emotional urgencies. Give yourself time to consider whether
that stowaway down below isn't steering your arguments
just as he steers much of the rest of your life. One of the
unhappy and depressing facts about students – or should I
say certain groups of students? – is the contrast between
their presumptuous intellectuality and the messiness of their
personal affairs. It is better to be unashamedly primitive
than to attempt to justify primitive behaviour with an
elaborate pattern of words.

If you have not had any sexual experience before you left
school you will certainly be tempted at the university, because you will be likely to meet other young men who are
intimate with girls, who will talk about it, and make you
feel inexperienced and inferior. You will at times find these
sexual activities talked about quite openly – there being a
sort of camaraderie in them, so that students help each other
to obtain the necessary privacy for the next adventure.

* This is indeed what I believe. There isn't space to argue the point
here, but I would say this; that Christianity has been far too much
thought of as a way of 'being good'. What we ought to ask is this: is it
true in what it says and implies about human nature and the consequences of actions?

142

TO YOUNG MEN - ESPECIALLY STUDENTS

This is an instance of the way doing a forbidden thing in a group makes it easier for the time being to avoid a sense of shame or guilt. Indeed, the action becomes shameless. Sexual activities encouraged and connived at by groups go to extreme lengths among students, fortunately a small minority, but nevertheless disturbing.

You may be of the shy or serious temperament that will keep you away from all these people; it is possible for students to go right through university life working hard and being quite unaware of the groups in which these things happen. But if you are socially adventurous you will almost certainly touch at least their fringe. You will perhaps be more likely to meet them if you are a member of an art school, a medical school, or a dramatic club than if you are a scientist, an English student, or a historian. This is not a lurid picture of 'Night Life in the University' painted in the Victorian manner to frighten you off vice. What I describe is what students have actually found in various colleges and universities throughout the country. I am not an old-fashioned moralist recoiling from a vision of sin. I am trying to be a sociologist and an educator, seeing the world as it is and asking what, if anything, should be done about it. Certainly I think that you, the student, should be prepared for what you will meet before you meet it. You should begin to ask yourself if you will be ready to make a wise judgement when the time comes to decide whether you will be drawn in or remain outside.

In so far as I make judgements about people's sexual life, I do not do it from a superficial concept of what is 'sinful'. I want to ask questions first, as a scientist should. What do people do? In what circumstances are they led to do it? Why do they do it - what are they seeking for? Do they really know what they are doing - all of what they are doing? What are the consequences? What is the effect on them - now, in ten years' time, in twenty years' time? Does the immediate pleasure leave a residue that spoils later years, a residue that interferes with marriage and family life? If there is suffering, who suffers most? Or is all this sexual activity a temporary commotion, a phase from which people emerge more or less undamaged, and ready for real responsibility?

I do not deny that I have feelings, and I find some of the more extreme activities repulsive; so indeed do most students when they hear about them. But I do not feel any sense of shock at the thought of two people who genuinely care for each other making love out of wedlock, though I do want to ask insistent questions about it.

We can never do things entirely of our own free will and from our own completely independent judgement. There are always fashions of thought which come and go and which subtly affect our thinking and decisions. We live in a climate of thought and it is only by making ourselves very conscious of what it is, and by a really disciplined effort, that we can become truly objective in our thinking. One of the current fashions is the emphasis on 'physical adjustment'. Here is an example of the way in which it may affect a relationship. Two students enjoy a friendship that becomes deeply affectionate. They are too 'sensible' to declare themselves in love with each other and to rush off to the Registry Office. They have read the many successors of Marie Stopes and, even more likely, the two weighty volumes of the Kinsey Report. They know the latest about orgasm and the importance of the lovers' being able to 'satisfy each other'. They know that marriage sometimes breaks up because the physical relationship doesn't work. So one, probably the man, says to the other: 'We can't know whether we are physically adjustable to each other until we try. What about it?' If the other consents they begin to sleep together when circumstances permit. The man will even go so far sometimes as to hint that he will not want to continue the friendship if they do not make this experiment.

Now do they really find, by this method, whether physical adjustment is possible; or rather, if they do not find that it 'works' does that mean that they are not really fit for each other? In a previous chapter I have pointed out the factors that make such an action unlikely to yield results that can be relied upon. Complete satisfaction for the woman may be quite possible but it may not come for a year or more. Will any student couple be likely to carry on the experiment for as long as that? Further, the anxiety in the girl to prove that she is all right is very great. It matters tremendously to her that she should prove a wholly satisfactory partner, that she should 'pass the test'. It is much more of a test for her than it is for the man; indeed it is often tacitly assumed in these experiments that it is the girl who is being tested. Sometimes a girl breaks down and cries in the middle of what should be a joyous and care-free experience because she feels that she is not coming up to scratch. It has to be faced that all these tests are necessarily carried out in unfavourable conditions, and that the very fact of their being consciously *tests* works against their success. There is much suffering in this sort of experiment, precisely because it is so insecure. The woman specially feels this. The situation is worse if the girl is aware that the man has had intimate relations with other girls, as is frequently the case. She fears that she will not be as satisfactory as the others were, and that he will once more pass on.

Having just mentioned it, I should put in a caution about the Kinsey Report, which has passed from hand to hand through the student world with great rapidity. It consists of two extensive investigations, one of the sexual habits of men and the other of the sexual habits of women, all in the U.S.A. A large number of men and women answered a battery of questions about their various experiences of sex — about masturbation, about intercourse before marriage, in marriage, or outside marriage, about its frequency at various ages, about the time taken over it, about orgasm — and so on. When it first came out it was freely said that it proved that women who had experienced sexual intercourse before marriage made more satisfactory wives. It proved nothing of the kind, for the report made no assessment of the *quality* of a marriage. The investigation was not of a nature that would allow such an assessment to be carried out, for it would have required a most intimate and sensitive inquiry into the daily conduct of each marriage and could not have been reached by mere questions. The Kinsey investigators dealt with thousands of people, so the questions could only be about what people *did*. Dr Kinsey was a biologist, not a psychologist or a psychiatrist, and he was investigating human *biology*. Unfortunately many people extended the implications of his discoveries, especially about orgasm in women, far beyond what was legitimate, and one can imagine they were prompted to do so in order to gain support for their indulgence in intercourse with girls whom they did not intend to marry. You can imagine how tempting the thought was: 'If Dr Kinsey is right, then the more sex experience I give this girl (or these girls) the better for her husband when she marries!'

Some of the psychiatrists who do have to investigate the intimate and personal aspect of marriage maintain that on the whole women who have had pre-marital intercourse are more likely to have unhappy marriages. In fairness it must be said that this, as it stands, does not prove anything. It does not prove that the pre-marital intercourse causes the unhappiness in marriage. In particular cases an inherent instability in the woman may cause her to be both wild before marriage and unhappy in it. All conclusions about human behaviour based on statistics should be looked upon with critical doubt.

To get back to our main theme, I have said that you may meet young men who are 'experienced'. They may carry an air of confidence, a knowing attitude, and they talk about 'having a woman'. Others will talk about their adventures in a half-miserable way, as though the activity were more of a problem than a pleasure, one in which they were seeking something they could never find. Some will seem genuinely pleasant and affectionate men, but men who do not know what they are doing. You will probably

not want me to spend much time on the confident irresponsible seducer, plainly unscrupulous, who prides himself
on the number of girls whom he has introduced to the
pleasures of sex. You will probably not be tempted to copy
him. Your sisters and your girl acquaintances are the
people who need to be warned against him, for he has a
technique and an experienced manner that go a long way
with an unperceptive girl and give her confidence in him.
All the modern emphasis on sexual techniques has made
girls afraid of beginners, who, they fear, will be bunglers.
An otherwise stable and sensible girl student was heard to
say: 'Yes, I would like my first experience to be with an
experienced man; it would be awful to be messed about
by one of these boys!' Probably she was influenced by the
amount of sexual activity among students that really is
'messing about' and is hurtful to the woman. But when
two 'inexperienced' young people meet in marriage and
are deeply committed to each other the whole quality of
the first experiments is changed, and even the difficulties
can be part of the happiness of the first few weeks.
They will look back on them with amusement and no
regret.

Now there is another sort of man, one whom you might
become. It is more difficult to find in him anything that is
plainly objectionable. He seems capable of good feeling and
can express some tenderness that is sincere. Perhaps for
lack of standards in his upbringing, or because he has been
exposed unprepared to some tempting situation, he has had
an early experience of intercourse with a girl student.
Neither he nor she had anything against it, so why not?
He didn't care for the girl sufficiently to want to go on
with it and deepen the relationship, but the experience was
enjoyable enough to make him look at other girls with an
appraising, questioning eye. What would it be like with her
– the next one? He is soon tempted to try. So he goes from
one to another, and perhaps makes no secret of his adventures. When he is challenged about his sexual adventures he may reply: 'Well, if the girls are silly enough,

why shouldn't I?' or 'If they are willing, what's wrong with it?' He is perhaps comparable to the sort of man you often meet in business, pleasant, charming, and friendly, who talks freely and without any conscience of the 'deals' he has pulled off. When examined carefully, as they are only rarely, the deals will prove to have been at someone else's expense and hardly fair to the other person. But it's the way people do business deals, so why not?

Here is a description, by a fellow-student, of one of these men, at a big city university where men and women mingle without restriction. 'He is fond of lots of beer, and indulges in much frivolous behaviour with the other chaps. Goes to bed with more or less any girl who is willing. He has a better relationship with one or two girls whom he respects, and with these, though he makes no secret of his desires, he does not press them. He still preserves, in spite of his promiscuity, the "ideal woman" illusion, and – frightful inconsistency – the romantic idea that the woman he marries must be a virgin although he has made short work of the virginity of a score of others. He is sensuous, can be kind and gentle, is on occasions outspoken and sincere and even generous. To women he is certainly lovable, dangerously so. But he is muddled, incredibly muddled. He talks, talks, talks – nonsense, stories, and work. We've all talked with him for hours, but no one ever gets near him, no one knows what he is really like underneath. He seems to be fumbling through his gregariousness towards a stable relationship, but has no concept yet as to what that could be like. He is quite incapable of turning his thought upon himself; he cannot examine or explain his own feelings.'

The sad fact is that men who have gone as far as this rarely pull themselves out of their muddled condition. They are not likely ever to be capable of depth in a friendship or of knowing what it might mean. Dimly aware of inadequacy, they go on from relationship to relationship in the hope of being one day fulfilled, filled-full, but they never are.

Among the men who go from girl to girl perhaps most are spoiled boys, egoists, men who are always the centre of their own worlds. In spite of their apparently deep interest in the opposite sex, they treat women as though they existed only to meet men's needs. A spoilt boy is one who always expects to get anything he wants just when he wants it; but as soon as he gets it he is not sure that he really wants it. All spoilt boys are egoists, but I'm not sure that all egoistical men are spoilt boys! Anyway, an egoist thinks of every experience, or feels about it, principally in relation to himself; he is concerned with how far it satisfies *his* needs, how much it matters to *him*, whether it is right for *him*. He may be a bouncing and confident type, seeming to sweep through life with all sails set. Or he may be a tense, preoccupied sort of man. The example just given perhaps fits the first type. Here is an example of the second.

'N. has had several girls in the last year or two and S. is his latest. She's deeply in love with him, but as always he doesn't know whether he wants her or not. He certainly doesn't love her enough to marry her, but he can't of his own will give up the affair. In the meantime she suffers terribly; she knows she is a fool to put up with him, but she can't help herself.

'He makes cynical remarks about other people's romantic illusions, but is a complete victim to his own. He wants satisfaction, perhaps even a deep satisfaction, but no woman ever seems to satisfy him once he has got her; he always goes on searching for the Perfect Woman, the woman who will give him all he wants. He can't see what women really are and that love involves giving. He is frightened — frightened of real women, of love, and of himself. He is lonely, because in spite of his continual thinking about himself and his feelings he cannot really *communicate*. The most distressing practical aspect is the fact that because S. doesn't satisfy him, he thinks he has a right to indulge in casual affairs while remaining doubtfully attached to her.'

There's an almost monotonous sameness about such reports; each description could fit a dozen cases and there are no doubt thousands of affairs among students following the same essential pattern. Whether there are more in the student world than elsewhere I do not know, but I'm inclined to think that there is much in the training of the bright boy that tends to make him a spoilt boy. So often he is the hope of the family, the one on whom its ambitions are centred, the one for whom money is saved. He may be excused domestic chores because his homework is so important. He hears himself spoken of with pride. Special attention is given him at school; his examination results receive public acclamation and through examination after examination he is groomed like a racehorse.

Remember that remark I quoted: 'If the girls are silly enough, why shouldn't I?' There is unfortunately a real basis for this remark. The girls *are* silly. This is the point at which it must be pointed out that women should recognize a large measure of responsibility for the way men behave. The mother who spoils her son is a silly woman. But unfortunately the silliness does not stop there. There are too many silly young women ready to continue the process when he leaves the apron strings. It is amazing how many young women can be caught in the egoist's net, swirled along with him for a while, then allowed to drift away injured. The half-miserable egoist gets one girl after another trying to meet his needs for him, and because he is always uncertain, chewing things over, with each girl the affair goes deeper and deeper as she tries to call on all her resources. When he leaves her for another, her distress can be ravaging.

Some of the seeming Don Juans of the student world, far from being he-men, are actually sexually inadequate, men who are not certain of their potency. They go from girl to girl, hoping that with each next one the experience will be so overwhelming as to convince them at last that they are fully sexed.

Why am I telling you of these various promiscuous types?

Do you belong to any of the types? If you feel you are missing something, recognize that the men who indulge in loveless copulation or brief affairs are not necessarily happy men, nor inwardly certain of themselves. They are not to be envied. It would probably be true to say that most of them find themselves more and more empty as time goes on, if they persist in their fruitless search. You can't indulge the body separately from the spirit without weakening the personality.

So far we have been thinking only of the men. But what about the girls? Is it really astonishing how little they are thought of, so deeply have we got it into our blood that women exist primarily to serve men. I have just been reading an interesting novel by C. P. Snow about a brilliant young Cambridge don, acute, witty, lovable, sympathetic, but without any conviction of purpose in life or even of any whole truth to which his own work might contribute. Between periods of great social activity he suffers from bouts of severe depression. He uses his charm to bring girl after girl into his net – or rather his bed: one or two semi-permanently, but scores for no more than a single night. The girls who know him well remain deeply, desperately, in love with him. As you read you cannot think him evil or even dislike him; you follow with interest and concern his spiritual struggle. You read the book to the end, to the point of his deliberately seeking and finding death in a bomber; you close the book, and then you wonder. What about the girls? Rosalind, Joan, the many he charmed, slept with for a night, and then forgot. What happened to them?

Isn't this book typical of our general attitude? There must be countless novels about the spiritual struggles of men, novels in which women come and go and are not followed up. They serve their purpose and are dismissed. Out of limbo and back into limbo. There is something about the whole of our society that encourages men – all men – to be spoiled boys and women to be their servants. I say this in spite of the fact that many women in the public eye – the film-star type – are obviously spoiled darlings who expect men to spend their time fawning on them.

What I want to suggest to you is that if you want to conduct your sexual life in a wholesome way you should accept completely, without any reservation, the spiritual and personal equality of men and women. It should be clear from my frequent use of the word *spiritual* above that I do not use it in a specifically religious sense. Joy and sorrow, exhilaration and depression, anguish, bewilderment, tenderness, compassion, bitterness, and despair – these are all experiences felt by the human spirit. When I speak of spiritual equality I mean the equal importance of these in both men and women. What happens to the woman in any sexual relationship you may have with her should matter just as much as what happens to you. 'Good heavens!' you may say, 'of course, if I loved a girl, what happened to her would be much the *more* important!' That is all very well in theory or in prospect. While actually engaged in loving, most young men are altruists. They would dive into a raging sea or rush into a burning building for *her* sake. But when the relationship breaks up, as all these relationships I have described break up, what then? In most instances the man deliberately hardens himself and blinds himself to what happens in the girl. He has to forget about her in order to be free; he has to find fault with her, to believe her inadequate, in order to excuse to himself his rejection of her. As for the cynically promiscuous, they *go into* an affair with the reservation that they are not going to be caught.

It is not easy for a casual observer, just by watching young people, to make a judgement as to who suffers most, the boy or the girl. In the more raffish groups of students the girls cover their feelings by a hard glitter, by excited behaviour, by artificial gaiety, by the flinging about of clichés or clever remarks that have an edge to them. The more sincere go and talk over their problems endlessly with their girl friends. There can be little doubt that in most of these affairs the girl puts more into the relationship than does the man. Because sex is so much part of her whole being, much more of her personality is involved, and she is stirred more deeply even though she may try to be casual about the affair. To carry on after the affair has ended she has to cover up and deny more of herself, pretend more.

If this is true, don't men owe it to girls to be specially careful and thoughtful as to what they persuade them to do? Is there anything at all in this love business that takes it beyond mere animal copulation? If there is, if consideration, sympathy, compassion, are not just emptily sentimental words, shouldn't love be as deeply concerned with what happens to her afterwards as it is with immediate pleasure? If tenderness is not just something that you turn on after you have turned off the light, shouldn't it imply a lasting responsibility?

Alas, human beings are not always thoughtful – not even students. They are not whole; they are made of bits that pull in different directions. They are often more disintegrated than integrated, and they do appalling things unconsciously, and take advantage of certain conditions without knowing what they are doing. If we are to be more the masters of ourselves and our actions we must understand more about the world of our time. We must understand the climate in which our thought and behaviour take place. One thing about the climate of today is, I think, very evident – the need that a girl feels to get a man. This does not necessarily mean – as the corresponding expression 'get a woman' means – to have sexual intercourse. Women want marriage, and that means not just sex, but a home, love, security, children, companionship. It is possible for fear to take hold of womankind as a whole, so that the need felt by each woman may become a desperate need. This happened after the First World War, when, because of the million men killed, there remained only three marriageable men for every four women. Women became acutely conscious of the danger of remaining unmarried, and I think this has affected every generation since. It persists into the present day even though there is now a slight excess of men.

This need for a man is related also to the need for *status*. In a society where men do the more spectacular things, girls tend to feel less important, less significant in themselves, than boys. So they want to achieve status in some other way. It gives a woman status to belong to a man, as his girl friend, his fiancée, his mistress, or his wife. The great significance a woman attaches to the married state can be seen from the fact that a woman who has achieved distinction in her profession will often after marriage prefer to be addressed as Mrs rather than by the doctorate she has earned. These two needs – the need for a man and the need for status – have a great hold on girls and profoundly affect their behaviour. I have heard it cynically said among students that a man no longer does the choosing.

The situation is made worse by certain ideas propagated and encouraged largely by men. One is the concept of the 'old maid'. The term is used with such ridicule as to suggest that the elderly unmarried woman is, of all members of society, the most frustrated and pitiable. The ridicule even percolates down into the teenage levels, when a girl who is shy, or who for some other reason has not picked up a boy, is called an old maid. It helps to create an atmosphere in which girls would rather have any man, yield to any demand, than be thought of as an old-maid-to-be. The ridicule is unjustified. An elderly spinster, provided she has worth-while work and lives in an ordinary mixed community, is more capable of looking after herself and is less to be pitied than an elderly bachelor in similar circumstances. I would warn you against ever using this cruel taunt to any girl or woman you know or may meet. Some girl students who do not get a 'boy friend' are made to suffer a good deal of unnecessary unhappiness through its being used in reference to them.

The American custom of 'dating' is perhaps the clearest indication of the impulses that move girls in the present-day climate. The girl who obtains the most numerous and frequent dates is a girl of great importance, and the need to get dates is a matter of feverish anxiety. Yet the dating has at first no immediate connexion with 'petting' or any other form of sexual activity. To go to the movies or for a walk with the boy friend is an adequate date as far as the total is concerned. It is obviously a matter of status first and foremost. But, of course, because this system – the terrible eagerness for dates – provides precisely the opportunity for male sexual activities, dating leads quickly to petting in later adolescence. What is regarded as status can be subtly altered by this. Many a girl has given in to a man because she wanted to prove herself a 'worth-while girl', or 'the right sort', and feared to be thought otherwise. I think it would be fair to say that until she is married and deeply roused by all that marriage means the desire for sexual intercourse is not very strong in a girl. The desire to be well-thought-of is far stronger, and it is this desire primarily that gets them 'into bed'. Men, therefore, who help to build up the pressures I have described and thus intensify their fears are doing something thoroughly unscrupulous.

But this is not the worst that men can do. It is not un- known in the student world for a man who wants a girl to yield herself to him – a girl who loves him, but is reluctant to go all the way – to use as a lever the threat of sleeping with another girl, and even to go and do it. Because of the desperate need to keep her man, the first girl, after all this, consents. Instances are known too, of a man being engaged to a girl in his home town and being intimate with her during holidays, and also having an unofficial girl at college or in his place of work and sleeping with her too. Both girls are aware of the full situation and both put up with it rather than risk losing the man.

In this book I am appealing to those who still have some vestige of a standard, some slight conception of what love might mean, to avoid any form of unscrupulousness them- selves and to do everything possible to alter this 'climate' of feelings and ideas that has put girls into such a slavish position. I am inclined to think, however, that there will be

13

SOME PRACTICAL CONSIDERATIONS

Now for a topic that has great practical significance – the use of alcohol. A woman went recently to a Marriage Guidance Clinic in the hope of saving her marriage. Though she loved and respected her husband, the marriage was in danger of breaking up because of her adultery with two other men. She was an able, interesting, and passionate woman, but there was an instability in her character, perhaps the sort of instability that would go with her qualities. It was not until she was closely questioned about the two adulteries that she realized the part played by alcohol in both. Both of the men, one of whom she knew, the other whom she had never met before, had made her 'tiddly' before suggesting intercourse.

I am not a teetotaller, but I cannot ignore the part played by alcohol in the degradation of sex. When I was a small boy in Battersea I used to see drunken men brawling in the streets on Saturday nights or lying inert in the gutter. Because this is no longer seen we might imagine that drinking to excess no longer happens; but it is a fact that drinking among teenagers and young adults has recently increased very greatly.* Drinking among students at dances occasionally reaches a stage where it is plainly disgusting and visitors have to leave because the whole atmosphere becomes unpleasant. There are too many college dances in which men are sick either in public or in the lavatory. In the 'good old days', while men drank heavily, it was thought unchivalrous and indecent to encourage a woman to get drunk unless she was of 'lower class'. Now equality is fully

* The police statistics show that between 1946 and 1954, for the age range 17–20, drunkenness became more than three times more frequent among males and nearly twice as frequent among girls. During the same period, sexual offenders doubled for both sexes.

established, there is nothing shocking in your girl friend being tiddly; and if a girl is mildly resistant it is not uncommon for a group of young men to see how much they can make her drink. It is after such an occasion that the suggestion is apt to come: 'What about ... bed together?'

There is further evidence of the all-too-tolerant attitude to which girls have been reduced in the way they put up with the sheer dirtiness and messiness of men. A man makes himself sick and helpless with drinking. His partner helps to tidy up the mess, sees him to his digs, perhaps even tucks him up in bed ... and greets him next morning with mild pleasantries. She would be doing him a greater service if she greeted him with five minutes of incisive language. I am sometimes for a moment bewildered when I ask myself how a girl, at a party or after, can allow herself to be kissed and cuddled by a man stinking of a mixture of tobacco, beer, and sweat. I suppose that is what is called 'an exciting male smell'. This of course gives the clue to it and tears away my last shreds of romanticism. It is a mistake to think that all girls are innately fastidious; some are only made so by propaganda, advertisements threatening rejection, and intensive education. In the moment of desire, their sense of taste and judgement may disappear. As the girl mentioned in Chapter 11 said, 'You just don't care. ...'

I have expressed myself strongly about the dangerous aspect of drinking at the risk of antagonizing the many students to whom drinking is an important occupation. But I do feel that if those who defend moderate drinking are to have any case against the militant abstainers, they must be able to show that drinking habits can be disciplined to reduce the dangers to negligible proportions. The two worst dangers are sexual depravity and road accidents. I want to continue to enjoy my sherry before dinner and my sampling of the wines of the countries I visit. I cannot do so with a good conscience if I remain silent about abuses. There is nothing kill-joy in this attitude; I am not asking for a dull sobriety, only that people should be in full control of their faculties when any serious decision has to be made. Over the years I have seen hundreds, indeed thousands, of young people hilariously happy, enjoying themselves in dances to the limit, without any assistance from alcohol.

What has been said about alcohol is true of drugs also. The 'hard drug' addict is probably beyond my reach, but readers of this book may well include takers of the less permanently harmful drugs of the kind fairly easily accessible, to students and even, alas, to young secondary school boys and girls. These drugs may provide relaxation, freedom from anxiety, or elation and pleasant hallucinations. I do not want to make emphatic generalizations at a time when there is doubt even in the minds of doctors and psychiatrists as to how these drugs compare with alcohol – which is also a drug – but I suggest that for present purposes the question must be asked: do they diminish the sense of personal responsibility? Would something happen between a young man and a young woman under the influence of drugs that would not happen otherwise? Does a drug diminish their ability to know and enjoy each other as they really are?

Some drugs actually reduce the desire for sexual contact, or the possibility of it. I have just remembered that Shakespeare recognized that alcohol, when taken in large quantity, has this effect. When the porter in *Macbeth* is asked by Macduff what three things does drink especially provoke, he replies:

Marry, sir, nose-painting, sleep and urine. Lechery, sir, it provokes, and unprovokes; it provokes the desire, but takes away the performance: therefore, much drink may be said to be an equivocator with lechery: It makes him and it mars him; it sets him on, and it takes him off; it persuades him, and disheartens him; makes him stand to and not stand to; in conclusion, equivocates him in a sleep, and, giving him the lie, leaves him.

But even were this so with all drugs, a problem would remain. Very often, drinking or drug-taking is an attempt to escape from reality; and the recent increase in both may be a result of the fact that to many young people our increasingly prosperous society seems increasingly purposeless and meaningless. Seeing in 'reality' no prospect of satisfaction, they turn away from it and seek a dream-world instead. But there is no escape this way other than a temporary one – unless you intend to enter the wholly lost world of the opium addict. You have to come out of the dream, or out of the relaxation or euphoria, back to the ordinary world; and your partner, your boy-friend or girl-friend, is part of that ordinary world; his or her faults, inconsistencies, unpredictable conduct, will have to be accepted and assimilated into your life: accepted in your clear-sighted sober moments, with tolerance and tenderness.

I have referred to equality, to the need for a full recognition of it in thinking about the effects of actions on men and women. I have also shown how the acceptance of equality has made it seem all right for a woman to be drunk. It looks as if it cuts both ways, doesn't it? It does, but there is no going back on it. If we are to avoid equality becoming equality in depravity, we must be definitely aware of the danger and we must fill out our conception of equality to make it complete. In any complete conception of equality, respect for the other person's integrity must have a dominant place; that will cut out any attempt to weaken the other person's moral control. I want to make it clear that in criticizing drink or drug-taking I am not trying to create conditions in which everyone will be led back to a rigid moral code. I do not believe that moral codes were pre-ordained by God and settled for all time, but I do consider that to break through the code is a serious action and that if it is to happen at all the two people concerned should be capable of normal judgement and should know, both of them, exactly what they are doing.

I think it would be wise for girls to be more insistent on financial equality – on paying their way instead of allowing themselves to be paid for. Every man knows what fun it is to take a girl out for an evening and pay all the expenses. But girls ought not to accept this unquestioningly in all circumstances and they ought to pay their way often enough to make it clear that they do not accept certain implications of the procedure, that they are not in fact to be bought. A nurse who had more strength of character than most reported: 'Just as I came off duty one night, a student whom I hardly knew joined me and took me down the road to a coffee bar for a drink. Afterwards he went with me as far as the nurses' home – and then I found that I was expected to go into the shrubbery with him and be extensively pawed. I'm sure if I had paid for my own coffee he would not have expected this.' Does this seem far-fetched? The girl concerned was far from being a prude and she was very perceptive. I think she was right. A good deal of the 'treating' of girls is a way of exerting power over them, and men are inclined to want power in more ways than one. They assume that they have rights. Girls are often trapped by this experience – not perhaps by cups of coffee, but certainly by an evening's entertainment. They are generous creatures and they find it difficult to be firm when a man says: 'What – stop now, after this lovely evening we've had together – I didn't expect *this*! Come on, my dear, be a sport.' It is, of course, the men that I am writing for at this moment, so what I should say is that generosity to a girl should be wholehearted; it should not ask for anything in return. If it expects sexual response from a girl who has no good reason to give it, then it is a contemptible fraud. If a man wants 'fun' at the end of the evening and intends to try for it, then he should not put the girl under any obligation.

Another suggestion that I should put in at this point is that girls should not be expected to behave all the time like dolls when they are taken out. I referred earlier to boys treating girls as though they were dolls that squeaked when they were squeezed. There are many refinements of this behaviour that are in essence just as trivial. An intelligent girl is often expected to behave like a simpering nitwit when a man is fussing round her, and because of this wretched tendency in girls to do what men want them to do, quite often they do descend in the presence of men to a shocking level of inanity and triviality. There is no reason why a girl should not express her sexuality with all her intelligence, her wit, and her imagination. I want to emphasize that in a sexual relationship people can get to know each other in an extraordinarily intimate way. This can apply – and should apply – to sex relationships at all levels, from going out for a walk together, or holding hands under the stars, to the intimacy of the marriage bed. It is perhaps the most fascinating and interesting of life's experiences. Much of the fascination arises from the differences. But even this experience of intimacy requires its own discipline, yes, even though we seem to be pushed along into it. Men must accept that an effort is required of them to understand girls, the same sort of effort and imagination that is required of any deep human study. This effort is impossible, and the understanding never achieved, if the friendship is maintained at a trivial level, and if men between them always discuss girls as though they were trivial and merely the objects of sexual attention. As one girl student put it:

Men don't understand that girls don't think and react in the same way as they do, and they don't recognize that making a personal relationship with a girl requires as much spade work as making a good friendship with one of their own sex. They pick up ideas from other men about girls being 'something extra in the hot-water bottle line' and don't see that that is not the whole story. Making personal relationships is the real problem; sex is secondary to it. Men are caught in the tradition that virginity is what you expect in the girl you marry, but all men should have 'experience'; because of this it is difficult to convince most young men that intercourse is not a necessary qualification for entry into adult life.

This brings us to the next practical consideration. How can you prevent a relationship with a girl from being swamped by sexual feeling and impulse? To begin with you must definitely intend that it shall not be so swamped, and that can only happen – the intention I mean – if you snap out of the traditional attitudes to women and begin to think of them as interesting persons who have something to give you that is not primarily sexual, something that is necessary to the whole understanding of life, something that has to do with human fellowship in every aspect. Next, you must avoid situations that are too tempting or provocative. I have already shown how alcohol can lead to a weakened control in which more primitive impulses take charge. But control can be weakened simply by circumstances, and it is wise to avoid those circumstances if it is desirable that complete sexual involvement should be avoided. It has to be recognized that almost any two young people of opposite sex who are reasonably attractive (and often even that would not matter) if put together frequently in circumstances that are intimate and private, will be impelled towards caresses and finally intercourse. This fact arises from the stuff we are made of, simply from our 'biology'. It need have nothing to do with any supposed evil in either of the two persons. Dr Marion Hilliard wrote a book* addressed to women which ought to be equally read by both sexes, every word of it. I cannot do better than quote some of it here.

Woman is equipped with a reproductive system which dominates her fibre. It has a vicious power that can leap out of control without the slightest warning, when a man and a woman merely share a companionable chuckle or happen to touch hands. Involuntarily the woman is twisted inside with anguish and longing.

When I was a younger doctor, caring for unmarried women about to have babies, I used to ask the more intelligent and sensible of them, 'How could this have happened to you?' The girl would answer simply, 'I couldn't help myself.' I was sceptical. I believed then, as most women do, that a woman controlled her relationship with a man. It became intimate because she deliberately chose to let it.

I'm wiser now and I know this isn't true. There can come a moment between a man and a woman when control and judgement are impossible.

A woman's first protection against this betrayal is to appreciate that the speed-up of her emotions is not only possible but natural and normal. Her best defence is to have no confidence at all in her ability to say nay at the appropriate moment. The belief that any woman can coolly halt love-making at some point before she is wholly committed is a tiger trap.

*A Woman Doctor looks at Life and Love by Dr. Marion Hilliard.

For this reason women have to safeguard themselves with a standard of conduct that may seem quaint and archaic. The freedom a modern girl allows herself is a delusion – it gives her no freedom of choice.

I have two reasons for quoting this. One is that the general thesis applies in a large measure to the male as well as to the female. There is a moment for him, however moral he may be, when he can control himself no longer. The second is that it is necessary to destroy the convenient illusion that it is the girl who in the final decision is expected to say how far, and that it is justifiable therefore for the man to go as far as he can. The girl is probably less able than the man to call a halt. Returning to my original question as to how to prevent a relationship becoming swamped by sexual desire, it must be clear that you must deliberately hold off and avoid physical contact in the early stages of getting to know each other. Reject the notion that as soon as you get to know a girl or have her as your dancing partner for an evening you have a right to kiss her. Most early kisses don't mean much and don't cause much, but later they may come to mean much more and by that time perhaps sufficient will have been built into the friendship for both people to be aware of what is happening to them and to be responsible for it. Sometimes, however, a single kiss is enough to throw the door wide open to sex. A girl who allowed herself to be kissed by an urgent young man for whom as it happened she had no respect, said afterwards: 'I felt a hot wave of feeling sweep over me against my will. But I'm glad it happened; now I know what to guard against in myself.' She was protected in this instance by the lack of respect; but the same thing happening between people who had some good feeling for each other would have precipitated the whole problem of sex and its control.

Next among these practical matters I must mention the problem of the 'neurotic' – the fear on the part of one that the other might prove queer in some way or other and therefore a poor partner in marriage. Neurosis is so much

164

talked about and written about now that it often comes into the thoughts of young people. In the purely sexual field, what they think of is the possibility of impotence, frigidity, or any other abnormality that would spoil experience of intercourse. I have mentioned in the previous chapter the present-day tendency for young people to think they must experiment in intercourse to find if they are adjusted to each other, and what I have in mind now is the fact that some people who get married do have difficulties because of a neurotic failure. How could they have foreseen these, and if they had, should they have avoided marriage and parted company? Would it have been better for them to have a 'trial marriage' first?

I cannot deal in this book with all the difficulties that might arise in marriage – but let us take a specific sexual difficulty that might be revealed in a 'trial', such as frigidity, or impotence. You must recognize that these are not likely to be isolated difficulties existing in an otherwise normal person. They usually accompany fears, inhibitions, obsessions, or twists of character that would be observable in the general personal relationship quite apart from sex. It is not necessary to attempt intercourse in order to find that something is wrong. If the two people really try to make something deep of their friendship, if they do not run away from the difficulties that arise between them, they will find out if there is a prospect of overcoming those difficulties. If a girl is going to suffer from frigidity in marriage it will be evident in fears and inhibitions about the physical relationship during intimate caressing, before any attempt at intercourse is made. It would be cruel to drive such a girl to the point of intercourse and to reveal her inadequacy in such distressing circumstances. If disturbance appears during the partial intimacies before marriage, they must be faced and dealt with at that level; they cannot be dealt with by forcing the intimacy to the point of intercourse. Fears *can* sometimes be relieved and dispersed by a loving partner, but never by urgency and forcing, only by tenderness and unending patience.

Remember that you are the product of your 'biology' and of the epoch into which you have been born. We all are, and we can cease to be slaves to inner and outer forces only by controlling their effects. The young man who says that it is now time to try intercourse, and gives fine reasons for it, is usually giving false reasons; his biological impulses are in fact the reason and he seeks a tolerable excuse for their indulgence. As for what we are born into, our epoch is so dominated by mechanical gadgets that we automatically tend to think of all difficulties as arising from causes that are technical – a matter of technique. Just as we look for the cause of an engine failure in a choked carburettor or a shorting plug, so we tend to think that a technical failure underlies an unhappy marriage.

Thank heaven the good life does not depend upon technique, upon calculation, and planning. It depends upon generosity, tenderness, sensitiveness. Given these, you can take problems of technique in your stride; without them, the most trivial of these problems will defeat you.

I need hardly add that there are plenty of couples who are well adjusted physically, whose sex organs work together very well, yet whose marriages are unhappy and who ought never to have become married. Their neuroses do not show in any immediate failure of sexual technique, yet they shatter marriage. To enjoy marriage and the continual presence of another person, you need to be free, free from obsession with yourself, free from that churning round of the mind by which it destroys its own energy, and destroys its ability to see interest and truth outside itself. We most of us go through a phase of this sort in the teens, caught in depressions that are self-produced and concerned only with the self. Nothing then has any meaning except as it affects *us*. We've got to grow up and out of this, or be well on the way before we get married. If there is any test that a couple should go through before they decide on marriage it should be a test as to whether they have this sort of maturity. They must know in themselves, and see in each other, that interest and energy and love are beginning to flow outward, that the springs of generosity are being released, not only into each other but into the world.

The world is difficult, but the mature person accepts its difficulties without resentment, without peevishness or petulance, without feeling that some obscure fate has its knife into him. He also finds his strength within himself, he is not dependent on his mother, nor does he have to exhaust other people in order to keep himself going. We all seek to escape from isolation into the companionship of marriage but, paradoxically, the best companion is the one who would, when necessary, have the strength to stand alone.

A great deal of publicity has lately been given to homosexuality, and you will perhaps be aware that there are a few men and women who seem to be fundamentally homosexual, attracted primarily to members of their own sex. It may be right to say that some of these are born with homosexual tendencies, but the opinion is strongly held among psychiatrists that most instances are due to a failure in upbringing, in the case of a boy something wrong in his mother's relationship with him. The effect of the relationship is unconscious and the young man therefore cannot himself understand the origin of his homosexuality.

It is normal for people to pass through a *stage* in growing up that can broadly be termed homosexual. Ordinarily they grow through this homosexual stage and out of it, later falling in love and marrying normally. A possible explanation of this stage in a boy is to be found in a reaction to his increasing sexual urgency. In puberty he begins to be acutely aware of the development of his sex organs and the strength of his sexual impulses. His own sexuality begins to disturb him, perhaps frighten him. So he turns away from girls; they are dangerous because they are the objects of sexual desire. He keeps company almost wholly with other boys. Sometimes the ordinary group life and common interests of the boys are enough for him; his 'homosexuality' may involve nothing more than enjoying the companionships and activities possible in the group. But commonly sex is much talked about in the group and homosexual acts may take place, instigated and encouraged by those who are more deeply homosexual in tendency. These acts will involve mutual stimulation of sex organs and perhaps attempts at a substitute for sexual intercourse.

In a mixed community the homosexual stage is short-lived and the boy soon begins to turn his interest towards girls, but if boys are kept apart from girls, as for instance in a boys' boarding-school, the homosexual stage tends to be prolonged and the temptation to homosexual acts becomes stronger. The impression I have gained after nearly thirty years' experience of co-educational boarding-schools is that in these schools homosexual acts are very rare. This suggests two thoughts. One is that if there are born homosexuals they are very few indeed; the other is that puberty and early adolescence form a sensitive period during which big personality changes may take place given suitable conditions, so that even a boy strongly conditioned towards homosexuality may fundamentally change. These are thoughts, not conclusions; the matter is one that requires more scientific observation, as does the whole question of homosexuality. Too many of the statements made about it at present are only opinions, often arising from theories too strongly held.

At present it is a fact that an adult who is deeply homosexual, either because of his bodily make-up or because of wrong treatment in his early family life, is very difficult to help. He cannot change himself by deliberately turning his attention towards girls. To attempt to work the homosexuality out of his system by experimenting with a girl would be grossly unfair to the girl; to expect her to marry him would be utterly wrong. A psychiatrist may be able to help, but at present his help may be more directed towards enabling the patient to bear his homosexuality and to live a useful life in spite of it, than to getting rid of it. No doubt many homosexual men will continue to seek sexual satisfaction with each other although their conduct is regarded by 'respectable society' as unnatural, however real the friendships may be. Most normally heterosexual men feel a disgust for homosexual acts and are as a result lacking in the understanding and compassion that the homosexual needs from the rest of the community if he is to be constructively helped. If he is not treated with compassion the homosexual becomes yet more of an outcast and is driven further into what seems to us perversion.

The brief homosexual stage in a boy's life need not concern us since it is normally innocuous and unremarkable. But if it is prolonged or involves much physical contact and stimulation it may create anxieties and inhibitions that will prevent the proper enjoyment of sex in marriage. It is not that the experience will turn the boy into a real homosexual; this is not likely to happen unless his earlier childhood has provided a basis for homosexuality; but it will leave a residue of guilt and a feeling of uncleanness spreading over the whole of his sexual desires and thoughts. A boy or a man in this condition is much easier to help than the type I have described in the previous paragraph, and he must not think of himself as homosexual. He may have enough spontaneous interest in girls to make a loving relationship with one, and if she is generous-hearted his guilt and anxiety may all evaporate. But if he feels deeply disturbed, or seems so to his friends, it will probably be wiser to consult a doctor or psychiatrist than run the risk of placing too great a burden on an unsuspecting and unprepared girl.

I have said that homosexuality is an inevitable tendency in some and a normal phase in others. This should not be made an excuse for acquiescence or irresponsibility. The innately homosexual man, however incurable he may seem, must be held responsible for what he does to other males, to the same extent as we hold the more normal man responsible for what he does to girls. The homosexual must not exploit boys or encourage acts that lead to degradation or perversion in society. Boys passing through the homosexual stage in the teens should remember that the impulse to exploit physical sensation – strong in nearly all of us – must be controlled so that the rest of the personality, their own and that of others, does not suffer.

There is one point that I must add to this all-too-brief discussion. Beware of using 'homosexual' as a cuss-word, a term of opprobrium. Deep and loving relationships often exist between men, and it is right that they should. There may be no physical impulse at all between them and their friendship may be wholly expressed in pleasure in each other's company, an enjoyment of each other's thoughts, and a sharing of common interests and activities. It is true that in certain systems of psychology this type of relationship is still classed as 'homosexual', but the word thus used is a means of broad classification, not a criticism of the relationship. In this sense I hope we shall all be homosexual as well as heterosexual. But to use the word – as many young people too readily do use it – in order to be suggestive and to cast doubts on the goodness of a friendship, should be firmly avoided.*

There is one further practical matter. If you recognize the strength of your sexual urges and you accept that you must not involve an ordinary girl in your attempts to indulge them, you may ask yourself: why not a prostitute? She is a professional, she has been through it all before. She will not be 'involved'. You release your tension without being too burdened with responsibility. You can learn about sex from someone who is prepared to remain anonymous and to make no further claims. This is a typically 'continental' argument. But what must happen in you if you are to use a prostitute? You must do without love; you must accept that the motions of loving are a counterfeit, a series of

*For a more extensive discussion of the problems of the homosexual, see *Towards a Quaker View of Sex* (Friends Home Service Committee, Friends House, Euston Road, London NW1, 3s. 6d, post 6d). This pamphlet is the report of an unofficial Quaker group, of which the author was a member, which attempted to understand, compassionately and without formal judgement, all kinds of departures from the conventional sexual code. It has stimulated a very interesting and equally objective response from a group of American Christians: *Honest Sex,* by Rustum and Della Roy (Allen & Unwin).

tricks that the prostitute has learnt, knowing the sort of sensations men seek. You must drive out of your mind the awareness that she has been 'had' by an endless queue of men, willing to use her as a hired outlet for their physical lust, that she has had completely to submerge her own fastidiousness in accepting man after man, irrespective of character, health, or cleanliness and having to endure from some of them perverse and cruel practices. Apart from the risk of disease, it is in fact possible that a few such experiences do little harm, and that men grow out of them to a more mature experience of love and sex. But once a man has seen what prostitution means from the other side – what it does to the women as they go on with such a profession into middle age with none of the consolations of marriage – then he could hardly encourage prostitution without injury to his own integrity.

Since the earlier editions of this book were printed I have learnt more about the circumstances in which unwanted or unintended babies are conceived. Borstal visiting has brought me into contact with many a young man who has caused a girl to become pregnant and subsequently married her or faced a court case. I have also been able to question several girls who have been heedlessly involved in intercourse. When I use the term 'Borstal' it must not be supposed that I am reasoning from criminal types. Most Borstal lads are fairly normal young men who are the victims of circumstances and group-attitudes; their conduct reflects conditions that are widespread.

Condoms are widely used by young men who have some intelligence, foresight, caution – or perhaps some feeling of responsibility. But there are also many who habitually assume that the girl will take precautions and wear a contraceptive; among these there are some who definitely consider it to be entirely the girl's responsibility. In a few instances I have been told by the young men that their church forbade them to use contraceptives; and when I said 'Yes, but what about the girl? You've made her pregnant!', the reply has been: 'Oh, that's her look-out.'

Some have been tripped up by a belief in the safe-period, and this leads me once more to emphasise that the safe-period method requires the most careful, intelligent calculation and a better knowledge than most girls have of their own menstrual rhythms. Yet others are superstitious enough to believe in good luck. Some statements, not made to me personally but reported, are to the effect that it is 'chicken' to use a contraceptive – implying that the hazard of making the girl pregnant adds to the adventure and that if you take precautions you are a poor thing.

I need make no judgement on the attitudes I have described; they can be assessed in the light of all that is said in this book about true equality and responsibility. But the need for clearer information is obvious. The intelligent reader who wishes to make himself or herself fully aware of the facts about contraceptive methods should read the *Report on Contraception* published at 10/- by the Consumers Association, Caxton Hill, Hereford, and made specially available to subscribers to the monthly magazine known as *Which*.

Many readers will be aware that birth-control has become a matter of urgent debate within the Roman Catholic Church, which has hitherto regarded any artificial method – i.e. any method other than abstention or the safe-period, 'rhythm', method – as sinful. It is known, however, that very many members of the Church use artificial contraception in spite of the ban. A rapidly increasing group of thoughtfully responsible Catholics wants the ban removed; they see suffering, neglect and delinquency in families too large to be cared for and the appalling dangers of over-population and world starvation, starkly presented in Sir Joseph Hutchinson's presidential address to the British Association for the year 1966. Because of its uncompromising attitude in the past, the Roman Church is now in a distressing and embarrassing situation. For a very moving description of both the difficulty and the sincerity of Catholic couples in their experience of modern marriage, Michael Novak's collection of thirteen reports should be read, called *The Experience of Marriage* (Darton, Longman and Todd).

14

LOOKING FORWARD TO
MARRIAGE

Do you look forward to it? Most of the romantic stories about young people end in marriage or the intention of marriage, but it does not follow that all young men who want sexual experience also want marriage. Some frankly want fun without any obligations. Others for a while believe themselves to be genuinely in love with a girl but cool off when she mentions marriage and go in search of some other girl who will not make that particular demand. Yet others are prepared to be faithful but can never be brought quite to the point of marriage. All these are instances of men who have persuaded the girls to indulge in full intercourse without marriage. What about those who do not go 'all the way'? Among these there will undoubtedly be many who look forward urgently to marriage because they want full scope for their physical impulses. Their physical urgency may be cloaked by the most romantic protestations and commitments, but fundamentally what they want is sexual satisfaction. These again – although they are prepared to wait for marriage – are men who want sexual satisfaction rather than responsibility.

All the above instances illustrate a marked difference between men and girls. Nearly all girls, whether they are conventionally moral or not, want marriage, a home, and children. The number of men who want these is by no means as great. I am writing about what I believe to be the conditions at the moment; they are likely to vary from one generation to another. I think there are today many un-happy instances of affairs in which the girl tries to get the man to commit himself, but the man with vague uneasiness, and perhaps irritation, puts difficulties in the way. From the point of view of the quality of marriage, neither the girl nor the man is behaving sensibly. As I have pointed out earlier, girls are over-anxious to 'get' a man, and this urgency is not likely to make for a good and lasting friendship. Friendship, which is the basis of all good marriage, is an experience that arises spontaneously; it just 'happens', without any desire for possession, getting, or holding. It happens because there are interests in common, because the two are at ease in each other's company. A man who is persuaded into marriage is not in a condition to make a good husband. On the other hand we cannot approve of the man who is prepared to grasp at the pleasures of love-making, to enjoy also the loving attention which a girl is often prepared to give to her man, yet refuses to give her what she desires and to accept the normal consequences of love-making.

These wrong attitudes belong to each other; each tends to produce and exaggerate the other. They are part of a widespread degenerate condition in sexual relationships.

The sort of love that makes a good marriage is of the same nature as the affection that exists in a good friendship; indeed it *is* the same feeling, but deepened and strengthened by sex. It is not primarily concerned with what can be got or enjoyed but with what can be given to the loved one. Several writers have pointed out that even in the sex act, when the body is full of exciting sensations, the deepest satisfaction comes not through what a man feels in himself, but through his awareness of the joy he is giving to the woman he loves. It is one of the great paradoxical truths of life that when we seek enjoyment for ourselves something goes wrong with it as we grasp it, whereas when we want to give the other person the greatest possible enjoyment, we incidentally become supremely happy. In the words of William Blake:

> He who binds to himself a joy
> Doth the wingèd life destroy.

Sex is obviously important in marriage, but it is not of *first* importance. Friendship and companionship come first, and it is only if there is a true foundation in these that sexual enjoyment will continue. In a love-affair there is at first a great deal of intense excitement. This is simply because the lovers are new to each other. Have you yet been for a holiday abroad – to France for instance? Perhaps you will remember your feelings as the boat approached the quayside at Dieppe or Boulogne – the curious excitement you felt as you saw, for the first time, the words above the shops beyond the quay or on the advertisements; the curious railway locomotives with all their insides outside, the blue-clad porters swarming on board, and the faint stimulating smell in the air of the different French tobacco. I hope you will never quite forget that first experience, but if you go frequently to France you will begin to take the differences for granted. That doesn't mean that you will cease to enjoy France: your enjoyment may indeed be deeper but it will have a different quality.

In the same way the quality of love-making changes. At first the other person is a foreign country. Exploring that country, physically and mentally, is an experience full of new and exciting sensations. But that stage does not last; and it is most important that when it is over there should be something more permanent to take its place. This should be the experience of knowing and understanding – corresponding to the experience you might have if you settled down in France, learnt how to use and understand French, and began to know the people from inside, so to speak. A very large number of young people, in spite of the evidence they can see in their own parents and other middle-aged couples, think that the early experience of being 'in love' will last for ever. Is it saddening to you that it must pass? But it does *not* mean that sexual enjoyment diminishes. The quality of the enjoyment does change: married people become familiar with the geography of each other's bodies; loving ceases to be the excitement of finding their way about. Each knows what the other wants and needs; knows better and better how to give the other what is wanted. Each one's body becomes more perfectly the instrument for expressing love and the body has more behind it to express. Using the body in love-making is like using a language. The man who settles down in France not only learns more French words but he has more to say. In a good marriage the body has more and more to say as time goes on and the couple go through more and more experiences together. A father of several children said to me recently, 'We've been married ten years, but we make love more often and we enjoy it more.'

If you want to be able to say that, ten years after marriage, you will have to make certain that your marriage is based on friendship and that it is undertaken because of friendship. That means that you must both of you enjoy each other quite apart from any excitement or pleasure you may get for yourselves; it means that you must be *interested* in each other. Many people in love are apt to think that the idea of being *interested* in each other is a queer irrelevant sort of idea. I think it would be safe to say that the majority of people in love are *not* interested in each other; that is why, after the first excitement has passed, the relationship breaks up. They are like the boy who goes to France in a school party, experiences those early excitements I have mentioned, but after a hectic scrutiny of shop windows and a sampling of pastries, is barely able to endure the Louvre and Versailles. He is soon ready to go home – clutching a model of the Eiffel Tower, just to show where he has been.

Falling in love is a very untrustworthy experience. Yet it is shown on screen and stage and described in books as though it were the only experience that mattered, and as though the more rapidly it happened the more it could be depended upon. Young people who really care about the future, who want a sound foundation for marriage, must be prepared to *control their sexual impulse*. This is not because sex is wrong but because once the sexual energy begins to flow in a relationship it is very difficult to take notice of anything else. Young people who think that 'sex is all right' and accept that it should enter immediately into a relationship in an uninhibited way, are making themselves incapable of seeing each other truly. It is better to have some inhibitions, to take it that you must wait patiently before you touch each other or talk of 'love'. When you see a girl who attracts you don't let the current fashion of thought drive you to think straight away of making love to her. Give yourself a chance to know her as a person first. And be fair to her; give *her* a chance. She would be glad to know that you thought her face charming or her figure exciting; but she would be even more glad to know – after a period of friendship – that you valued her as a person, that you knew her through and through and yet loved her. It is good to be able to tell a girl that you not only love her, but *like* her. How many young men can say that, and mean it?

A good marriage is not easy to achieve. You cannot automatically become a good husband any more than you can automatically become a good scientist, a good poet, or a good cricketer. It requires preparation, training, knowledge patience – a willingness to discipline yourself in order to achieve your aim. Many people who have been long and happily married have become so attuned to each other that they forget that they ever controlled or disciplined themselves. Perhaps the word 'discipline' is frightening. What is meant is largely the discipline of humility and compassion – the willingness to look into yourself when things go wrong, and admit yourself at fault, and the readiness to *feel with* the other person.

Because you take your whole self into marriage, your whole life is a preparation for it. You will not be able to be humble, to express tenderness, to feel compassion in marriage if you have not already felt and expressed these in your everyday contacts, in your friendships, and towards the people with whom you work. Merely falling in love with a girl will not make you a different person from what you are already. Almost any man will find himself expressing the tenderest of feelings as he caresses his beloved in the dark, but if he is not already, and essentially, a tender and sensitive person, cruder and harsher feelings will certainly break through under the stress of marriage. Marriage does make heavy demands upon human personality.

Let us suppose that in your everyday life you have been reasonably thoughtful and that your feelings and actions have been sorted out and well directed. You are now entering upon a friendship that might lead to marriage and you are wisely holding back sexual demands in order to give friendship a chance. What is there that you have to discover? Chiefly it is this: whether you are agreed about the things that matter most in life, whether you are both fundamentally at one, whether you are likely to stand together in any crisis that life may present.

Every young man should be aware of an all-pervading weakness in girls – the tendency to let love, or what they think to be love, swamp all considerations of social outlook, politics, religion, ethics, and indeed anything else. I have referred to the irresponsibility of young men who want fun without marriage and have contrasted it with the desire of girls for marriage and children, but I do not blink the fact that the girls' desire may be primitive, blind, undiscriminating, and unscrupulous. Many a woman will shelve her religious or political convictions in order to marry the man she 'loves'. To put it more politely, a woman is all too prepared to make 'adjustments' in her outlook in order to make marriage possible. I have heard it argued that it is just as well that women should be able to make adjustments of this sort, for otherwise how would the majority of marriages survive? It is true that many marriages are kept in existence by the adaptability of women. But a marriage of this sort is always a second-best. It is not a *unity* of active, searching, completely honest minds.

It has been estimated that not more than ten per cent of marriages are really creative. A creative marriage is one in which each partner is made more active, more keenly alive in every way by the presence of the other, a marriage in which one-and-one make more than two, a marriage in which the couple make a distinctive contribution to their community that they could not have made apart.

If you are to get to know the mind of your girl friend you must see to it that you do not do all the talking and that she does not merely agree with you. Do not assume that it is the man's job to make all the major decisions. Do not be afraid of disagreement; no two people ever got to understand each other without some disagreement. But if you find yourselves in disagreement about fundamental matters, do not try to find an easy way out. Do not bear her down with argument or demand her loyalty. The matter must be thought right through, without pressure or persuasion, until you reach a real agreement, or until you recognize a fundamental difference of outlook. If you recognize this it may be wise to put aside all intention of marriage or sexual contact. Although it might be possible to live through the first few years of marriage without serious conflict, the advent of children and their education are likely to bring the hidden disagreement to light in a painful way.

It is not so much opinions that I am thinking about, for people's opinions may change a great deal in the course of years. It is more a matter of values* – the deep valuations and feelings that direct people's lives, especially when they have serious decisions to make and crises to face. Don't forget that feelings are more important than ideas, statements, thoughts, opinions. Feelings are at the bottom of our judgements. It is the ability to feel together that enables people to stand together.

Feelings, like statements, can be rational or irrational, true or untrue. It is irrational to be afraid of a burglar under the bed when you know that he cannot be there. It is irrational to feel overwhelming love for a girl, just because you are full of sexual urgency, when you do not really like her. It is a true feeling if you are afraid of a man who threatens you with a gun or if you love a girl whom you know well with all her faults and virtues. Growing up is largely a matter of developing true feelings and getting rid of untrue feelings, secondhand feelings, irrational feelings.

*See page 132.

Often people who are in love with each other find a welter of irrational feelings bursting up into their minds. Jealousy where there is no real occasion for it. An intense feeling of hurt when a serious statement of feeling is taken casually. A fear of anything that may make claims on the other partner. A desire to be the sole preoccupation of the other.

It would be too much to ask that young people should free themselves from all irrational feelings before they get married, but I think they should prove to themselves that they can do this in a few situations. Suppose that they find that in a lovers' quarrel they cannot do this, that they merely wait for it to simmer down and hope to forget it, or that they try to obliterate the conflict by love-making. Then that is a failure. But if they come through it in a way that makes them feel they know themselves and each other better than before, it means that they are growing up together and have reason to be confident.

A young man should never tolerate a girl who, in times of difficulty, tries to play emotional tricks with him, seeking to avoid the issue by manipulating his feelings. I have already shown that there are times when a girl should turn her back. There are also times when a man should turn his.

I have emphasized, perhaps rather grimly, the dangers and difficulties, the things that may go wrong. It is worth while to face these precisely because a marriage that is a right marriage, a marriage of true minds, is such a transcendent and transforming experience. It is worth while doing everything possible to earn such an experience. I want now to turn to the positive side – to the things that can be enjoyed in a friendship that might lead to marriage and in marriage itself.

An intimate friendship can be a wonderful experience of growth, leading to a great increase of knowledge and sensitiveness. I mean knowledge of the world around, a keener appreciation of all that life has to offer. Much of the effort of teachers to educate children is unsuccessful because there is no intimacy, no acceptance, between the teacher and the boy or girl. If the teacher points to an object or a line of poetry and says that it is beautiful, the pupil is quite likely to reject the idea because he does not want to share that teacher's experience, however genuine it may be. But a young man and a girl can introduce each other to a whole range of new experiences. If they really care for each other they will want to share experiences; they can do for each other what their teachers perhaps failed to do. But there must be willingness that this should happen. It is just not good enough, for instance, if a scientist falls in love with an artist and each is content to allow the other's interests to remain a mystery.

Besides sharing what they already have they can make discoveries that bring something new to them both. Intimacy should make them more sensitive to everything than they were before, and going about together should be an opportunity to see much more of the world around them, to become more sensitive to its beauty and its ugliness. It is a time to develop taste and discrimination, to make new judgements about books, furniture, pictures, architecture, music, to investigate politics and religion, and to begin to understand the need for a community. Some couples can look back with delight upon the year or two that preceded marriage precisely because that time was so full of these mutual activities, interests, and discoveries.

It should also be a time when children and education are discussed. Within a year of marriage there may be a baby, and education begins from the moment a baby is born. What happens to the child before it goes to school usually matters more than anything that happens afterwards, and both young men and women should prepare their minds for the responsibility.

I am not taking it for granted that the young man and woman necessarily get married. It may be that they decide not to, and I have therefore not referred to them as an engaged couple. Even if they do not get married the experience will have been of great value. A broken-off love-affair should never be thought of as a 'dead loss' and there should be no deliberate attempt to forget. Everything should be remembered and made part of wisdom.

Now what about marriage itself? What is the nature of marriage? What is it for? Very many people – including some Church people – will answer that marriage is for the procreation of children. That is in fact a very irreligious answer. It is merely the answer of a biologist. It is an answer that could be made with complete conviction by a Nazi. Human beings are much more than breeding animals, and when two people commit themselves to marriage they are not necessarily committing themselves to procreation. They are committing themselves to a joint search.

This is my view and it may seem a particularly individual point of view. It must be explained. It is not just because I am a scientist that I see life as a search. It is even more because I see how children behave and what brings them enjoyment. I have seen my own two children, as well as hundreds of other people's children, making their early attempts to explore the world around them. I have seen them full of curiosity, heard them ask question after question. I have seen them make discoveries and find the answers to their questions. I've seen in them the joy of achievement, the satisfaction of really knowing all – or nearly all – about something, as a result largely of their own efforts. I have watched boys and girls making experiments, not only in the laboratory, but also in the art room, the workshops, and at the piano. I have watched a child, after his early frightened attempts to swim, at last trust himself to the water and shout 'I can swim'! I have known many children discover music for the first time and revel in the rich new experience that it brought to them.

Now in all this I see something absolutely fundamental to human life – to our enjoyment of living. It is searching, finding, adding experience after experience to the pattern of our lives, seeking for a meaning in it and enjoying the richness of it all – that is what makes life worth while. I would add that this is a religious search and in its wholeness brings a religious satisfaction, but I am always wary of the people who think of religion as an idea that you have to accept. To me it is the search itself and the discovery it brings.

I see life in this way and I see marriage as part of this universal activity. Human marriage – as distinct from animal mating – is not functional; it is not primarily a way of getting something done. It is not a way of settling down. It is a decision to share an adventure, to pool knowledge, resources, different sensitivities, and temperaments in the search, to share the discovery and enrichment that result. You don't know where this sort of marriage will lead you – but you do know that, wherever it takes you, you will not be alone, and life will not be dull.

You will realize how important this is when I refer back to the young men who avoid marriage and the girls who desperately want it. To get a husband and a home and to have a baby is simply not good enough; that in itself is no more than rabbits do. Whether it becomes a creative experience, something fully human, or just a dull functional activity, depends upon whether you think of marriage as a new freedom, an opening up of the whole of life, or as a withdrawal into a material security. There is no point in breeding babies into dullness, into what Priestley calls an Admass culture, an Admass civilization.

The nature of marriage should be such that you – a young man of adventurous spirit – can go into it without feeling that your adventures are at an end and that you are going to be restricted and confined by new responsibilities. You will have the adventure of getting to know *her*, and that should involve some surprises. You will fail to have this happy experience if you go into marriage thinking that you know all about women and how they behave. You must be prepared to find that you know very little. Then there is the adventure of planning a home and designing its contents. There will be little pleasure in this if you wait until you have a big income and can spend lavishly, or if you slavishly accept the popular taste and furnish your home from the dull packing-case styles that fill the hire-purchase shops.

There is great fun to be had in going to auction sales and learning to distinguish between the good and the bad. You can furnish your home at very small cost in this way, instead of remaining indebted to a furniture firm long after you have become sick of the sight of that three-piece suite. If you can use a saw and a plane there is even more interest to be added to the adventure of getting married on very little money.

Children? Having children can be a form of self-indulgence or it can be a fascinating experiment. If you think of a child as an extension of your own personality, if you decide in advance what its sex will be, what temperament it should have, what school it must go to, what opinions it should acquire, and what career it should follow – then indeed it will be a dull experience. But if you are prepared to care unpossessively for your child and just see what happens, you will find fatherhood intensely interesting. Men – and expecially boys – are apt to think of young babies as all the same, until they get to the point of running about, making things, and talking fluently. But in fact the amount a baby learns in its first two years is perhaps the most astonishing fact in the whole of nature. A man who is prepared to observe what happens – and to share the duties involved in the care of a baby – will have no reason to feel that marriage shuts out the interesting things of life.

It is a delight to watch a young child learning. A few days ago I was visiting a young family, and the youngest, a girl of fourteen months, was just learning to walk. At one point she bent over to touch the floor with her forehead and accidentally somersaulted. After that she performed somersaults all over the floor for half an hour. The interest you can find in watching this sort of thing can continue right through your child's life up to adulthood. But it will continue only if you look upon your children as distinct and independent creatures, growing up in their own way to stand on their own feet. If you make up your mind in advance about them and you think you can 'mould' them, you will only be disappointed, and fatherhood will become a dull, burdensome experience.

I nearly said, a few paragraphs back, that an interesting creative marriage would not lead to a dull little house in a street full of dull little houses in suburbia. I realized that it *might* lead to that. Would that be the end of adventure? Not necessarily. It is possible to make an outwardly commonplace little house a hive of activity and a centre of life not only for the people who live in it, but for many in the neighbourhood. Millions of people have to live in such houses in the dreariest of housing estates. If their minds were conditioned wholly by the houses they live in, a very large proportion of them would be doomed to stagnation; but the human spirit can break out in the most unpropitious surroundings. Nevertheless, young people in early adulthood do want to move around, to see the world, to sample the jobs it offers, and you should not think of this activity as necessarily coming *before* marriage, and of marriage as putting an end to it. There are plenty of young women who are prepared to move around the world with their husbands, and among the children I have taught there are many who were born in remote corners of the earth. A few months ago my granddaughter was helped into the world by a black midwife in Ethiopia. The rapid extension of medical facilities all over the world has made this sort of experience little to be feared.

Don't confuse the real adventure of marriage with the process of 'getting on'. Marriage soon degenerates when it becomes a matter of competing with the neighbours – when you feel you have to put the baby in ridiculous ribbons and frills in an immaculate perambulator in order to keep your end up; when you feel you must have a car as good as the one next door, or are afraid to be left behind in the upsurge of T.V. aerials. The happiest, most interesting, and charming young couples are usually to be found in houses where the furniture is not so glossy that the children dare not romp, where the lino is very worn, and the car much more than secondhand, if it exists at all.

Now what about the everyday problems and adjustments of marriage? The most familiar phrase that comes to mind is 'give-and-take'. But of all the descriptions of what marriage should be it is about the dullest, the most sterile. It is a fact that when happily married people *look back* on their time together they are aware that there has been give-and-take – that is, forgiveness, tolerance, patience, making allowances. But it would be fatuous when looking *forward* to marriage to think of basing it on this. If you are a forgiving, tolerant, patient person, you will express these in marriage; you won't need to *decide* to do so. If you are unforgiving, intolerant, impatient, your marriage will be in trouble very quickly; indeed if you are all this you most certainly should not get married. Now we are none of us anywhere near perfect, and no one should wait for perfection in himself or his partner before getting married. But perhaps it would be right to say that everyone getting married should be able to say to himself that he is, for instance, becoming more tolerant, more patient. In marriage it is not the possession of virtues but the capacity for *growth* that matters. If you have that capacity, then your marriage-conflicts will not be misfortunes, but opportunities, because you will learn from them; they will take you a step ahead.

If there is one great fault that stands in the way of a good marriage it is pride. A proud man cannot learn, because in order to learn anything you must first admit that you don't know. If you are too proud to admit your ignorance you will always remain ignorant. If you persist in thinking that you are a fine chap you will never become one. If you always think you are right you will nearly always be in the wrong. The way to knowledge is through humility.

Marriage provides the best opportunity for humility. Your wife should be the very special person whom you will allow to know you as you really are, and therefore the one person who can most help you to go on growing. You can do the same for her. No matter how much of a damned fool you have made of yourself, she is the one person who can be told about it. Love does not depend upon your being a fine chap, it depends far more on your being humble and honest. Human beings are nearly always lovable when we know them intimately, even though grave weaknesses are exposed. What makes people unlovable is a false covering – a shell, a mask, a stage-outfit. It is tragic that among the nonsense associated with the romantic view of marriage there is the idea that your partner in love is the person to whom you must above all be admirable. People nourished on this idea cannot be honest with each other. They live together like actors, until the stage collapses.

I hope you will see that the idea of marriage that I have been giving you is one that is wide-open, in no sense closed-in. You can't wrap it up in slick phrases such as give-and-take, adjustment, team-work, not even unselfishness! There is no 'technique' for successful marriage. People who get married should enjoy each other – enjoy each other's presence, each other's mind, each other's temperament. They should know that they would enjoy each other even if they could never touch each other. They should know that they want to enjoy life together – not just enjoy each other within four walls, but enjoy looking out on the world together and doing things in it, learning from it. And – this is very important – they should want to enjoy people together, to be part of a community of fully-shared friends.

Such people will not want to plan exactly what their life will be together, they will not become the victims of trivial or grandiose ambitions. They look outwards at the world and they care about it, and because they move forward courageously into life they do not know what will happen to them. What they will discover and create will become clearer as they experience life together.

I put all this before the question of having children because if the conditions of a marriage are good the partners inevitably want children and they will be fit to have them.

Now for a last thought that may seem an anti-climax. Food and cooking! This is not a descent to the ridiculous; it is exceedingly important. If you are thinking of marrying your girl friend, make sure that she is interested in cooking. If she isn't yet, then do your level best to make her. If you want some fun before marriage – fun which no one could possibly take exception to – then learn to cook together. I say *together*, because a husband who develops discrimination, taste, and adventurousness in cooking will be a great stimulus and encouragement to his wife. Learn to cook every sort of omelette, how to grill steak exactly right, how to make an old hen like chicken. If you can't afford these, learn how to make cheaper things attractive. It can be done. Find out about sauces (the French say that the English know only one sauce – custard – and we drown everything in it!) and discover how to make vegetables a delight instead of a smelly sodden mess. Don't base your taste on tinned foods. They tend to create a deadly standard-ization, and they are expensive. If you want ideas, get a copy of Raymond Postgate's *Good Food Guide*, and take your girl out to a meal at one of the recommended restaurants – not necessarily an expensive one – and choose unusual dishes.

I'm not joking; I'm very serious. So much has been written about the technique of love-making, but it seems not to be realized that whereas married people may make love once or twice a week, they have to eat three or four meals a day. Eating ought to be a delight; high thinking and noble aims ought never to be an excuse for dull and inedible food; and passionate embraces are never a substitute for a good meal. The fact is that food isn't simply *food*, it means much more than physical nourishment. The birthday cake that a mother bakes for her child is a tremendous symbol of love, and the better the job is done the more love it expresses. Grown-ups need this expression just as much as children do. There's no harm in telling girls that the way to a man's heart is through his stomach. It is not the whole truth about marriage, but she's a foolish woman who neglects that route! This is not being materialistic. The good things of the earth – sex and food included – are for the enjoyment of man and the glory of God; and fortunately for humanity, God does not deny that enjoyment even to those who are unaware of him.

Further, every meal ought in a measure to be a celebration, a celebration of the common life, of the underlying unity and faith in marriage and family. The quality of the food should be worthy of such a meaning. The experience is, in a sense, a form of love-making and love-making in the more specific sense is at its best when it is not an isolated act but is continuous with family experiences which have the same underlying meaning.

But you – the husband if you become one – must not ask all this of your wife as a right. It is something you must make possible together. When you come home you must not plead that terrible day at the office. You must expect to bath the children and put them to bed while your wife puts the finishing touches to the evening meal. You'll be all the better for it; children are a wonderful antidote to the cussedness of adults. And don't forget the washing-up afterwards; share it.

SEX AND RELIGION

ONLY at rare intervals in this book have I allowed myself
to disclose that religious convictions have anything to do
with my views. My reluctance springs partly from my
memory of the mixture of religious instruction and misguided sexual advice that was offered to young people when
I was a boy. Perhaps much of what I have said would be
supported by people who have a knowledge of the facts of
human behaviour but no religious faith, people who consider that a rational system of ethics is adequate. But I do not
consider that a system of ethics, however sensible and good,
can be adequate. There can be a very big gap between
thinking something to be true and putting the truth into
action. You must have come across instances, in other
people and in yourself, when a very clear truth that
obviously needs to be applied in a particular situation
nevertheless leaves the person quite cold; it seems to have
no *energy* associated with it. When *does* the truth about personal behaviour carry conviction and energy? Isn't it when
that truth comes through some person you know, through
that person's conduct and experience?

I know how true it is in science teaching that a good
experiment is much more convincing and appealing to a
pupil than reading or talking about the truth it demon-
strates. A human being acting truly has a tremendously
greater impact on us than discussions about what our conduct ought to be. I believe that science and religion are far
closer together than most people think; in both of them,
truth is most complete in *action*. Ideas are secondary.
Religion, or should I say the religion that I and most of my
friends care about, is concerned deeply and fundamentally
with what happens between one person and another, with
the mystery of friendship and love, and their transforming

190

power. This religion must have a person at its centre; nothing less will do, no dogmas or rules or pseudo-scientific notions will suffice, for these are all thoughts produced by persons and therefore less than persons. Nothing less than a living person can give us the complete truth about humanity. That is why the person of Jesus is so significant. If I have any conception of God – otherwise an incomprehensible mystery – it is through him.

To love a person – husband or wife or friend – is I think the most satisfying of all experiences; it seems supremely what we are made for; nothing else is so meaningful, however incapable we may feel of expressing that meaning in words. It seems to me logical that if we are to go beyond our immediate experience of those we love to find some essential truth about our existence in the universe, it must be something that includes this most meaningful experience of our lives – it must be truth *in a person*. Whatever God is, there must be a Person in his mystery.

This thought will encounter strong resistances in many people – especially those whose experience of love has been unhappy or trivial and passing. Others cannot accept it because the scientific search for truth occupies their minds exclusively. They think of the vast material universe, its immense expanding distances, of spiral nebulae, hydrogen condensation, cosmic rays, and short-wave radiation. If they think of it as a mystery, it is a cold impersonal mystery. They forget that there is another mystery – the mystery behind the eyes of another person. If the material universe is tremendous in its extent, endless in its possibilities of exploration, so also is the world inside the minds of the people who sit beside us, every bit as mysterious and fascinating. I don't mean fascinating in the way it is seen by a psychologist but as it is experienced in the warmth of friendship and love. This warmth is as real as any of the particles of physics, indeed far more unchanging, and it is as dependable and eternal a truth as Einstein's $\varepsilon = mc^2$ may prove to be. If the heart of the universe is warm, there is a person at its heart – God.

To me Christianity is the truth about persons* and what happens to them. I have only the vaguest notions about God apart from Jesus, but in so far as the life of Jesus has made me aware of what God is concerned about, it seems to me that it is what we do to each other, do with, and for each other, at every level of our relationships. People get into difficulties, they injure each other, they turn their backs on truth, they make horrible mistakes, and find themselves in tragic situations. That is what life is like, and Christianity is closely concerned with what we do about it all. Its message is essentially hopeful. No situation merits complete despair and abandonment. An evil situation is a challenge to all our resources and we are so constituted that we can encounter and deal with evil, and grow in stature as a result. Christianity does not state that we can avoid the consequences of evil, but it does say that we can lose our fear of the consequences and we can prevent ourselves from being destroyed in spirit. The extraordinary power in men and women by which they conquer fear and redeem an evil situation is called by Christians the Grace of God, which means the help of God. There are people calling themselves Christians who speak as though the Grace of God were available only to professed Christians. This is very mistaken; it would be a fantastic contradiction to imagine that a loving God would limit his help to those who went through a particular ceremony or assented to a particular statement or belief.

Anyone who has humility and who knows what it is to be deeply and constantly loved by a spouse or friend will be likely to say or feel 'I do not deserve this. I haven't earned it; it is a gift.' But from whom? Not only from the other partner, for both feel that something has come into their

*I am using the word *person* in an entirely different sense from its use in the Christian Creeds. The 'three persons' of the Trinity are different aspects or presentations of God's activity, person in this sense being derived from *persona,* a mask used in a play or the part played by an actor. The modern use of the word refers to the wholeness and uniqueness of a living being, almost a reversal of meaning.

lives that, as a pair, they did not deserve or earn. Both receive more than they feel worthy of and both give more than they imagined themselves capable of.

Love *is* an overwhelmingly generous experience, bigger than any of those things we achieve by hard work or ability, such as business success or academic distinction. Those two rewards we can perhaps without too much pride say that we earn, but love is not of that nature at all. There are many people who repudiate the idea of anything transcendent or mysterious in life. Some of them would no doubt want to put love on a level with the other rewards, but I would say that such people only provide an example of the way in which, as Erich Fromm points out, people have allowed the commercial attitude to penetrate into the most intimate recesses of their spirits. Think of a young man saying: 'I worked tremendously hard all last year; I got my degree and I reckon I deserved it.' We should not think any the worse of him for making such a statement. But what if he said: 'She loves me with all her heart, and I reckon I'm worthy of it'...?

I would not say that this generosity of the gift of love *proves* the working of God in our lives, but those of us who have some belief in God feel that this mysteriously generous incoming is made possible by the Grace of God. It can happen to anyone.

It would be ridiculous to assume that it does not happen to people who are not Christians; but I would however say that it is worth while to try to penetrate to the central meaning of the life of Jesus because then we can learn how to call on the help of God when we consciously need help. Even those who have experienced this spontaneous generosity of love will have to meet difficulties, and there is no doubt that most marriages have to pass through crises more or less severe. People are often terribly shaken by these crises and it is certainly true that more often than not they are inadequate to deal with them alone; they are simply not strong enough. They need to search or wait for greater patience, wisdom, insight. It isn't just reason or logic they need, but a new sensitiveness coming into the deep parts of their minds where reason and words have no place, an incoming enabling them to 'rise above themselves' by a power that seems greater than their own.

This sort of experience generally comes to people slowly. They are not transformed overnight, but become aware bit by bit of something happening to them that enables them to cope more wisely and sensitively with crises. The picture of perfection that religion has so often held up before men and women has rarely been helpful. People are so different from this picture that the tendency is either to reject religion as alien to their experience or to feel hopelessly convicted of sin, to feel worthless, a condition specially created by sexual conflicts. Think of the way in which ideas about Jesus have been used in an attempt to deal with a boy's impulses to masturbation and sexual thoughts. The result in most instances has been to make the boy feel that Jesus was such a 'pure' character that he had nothing in common with him.

Such a concept is a perversion of Christianity. True Christianity is *not* a religion for perfectionists. It is true that Jesus said: 'Be ye perfect...', but the original Greek word did not mean what we most often mean by perfect; it meant something more like mature, grown up, made whole. Becoming perfect in that sense does not mean becoming free from faults, keeping all the rules, living an exemplary life and being a uniformly 'good boy', a condition that is both impossible and undesirable.

This is a very difficult point to make clear. I do not mean that we should not try to be better than we are; but we cannot do that by fitting ourselves into a pattern of goodness. Living according to a pattern doesn't help us in the complicated personal situations of everyday life. Finding and obeying the will of God in each particular situation is quite different from applying rules or 'being good'. Christianity recognizes that life is a fluid changing experience in which joy and sorrow, wisdom and error, success and failure, love and hate all are passed through. It is more concerned with what does happen than with what ought to happen. It shows us what we can make of our experiences whatever their nature.

Christianity is not an ideal, a faith to be practised some time in the future. It is not a way of avoiding difficulty. It is a way of living in an imperfect and difficult world, of interpreting experience of every sort, of digesting and assimilating experience, being nourished by it.

Jesus was not an ideal, though the Church seems to have done its best to make him so ideal as to be remote and colourless. He did not fit into anyone's idea or ideal of what he ought to be. He was on the contrary intensely real, provocative, and unexpected. It is important to remember what kinds of people Jesus consorted with, the people who made up his community. These people included the outcasts, the despised, the publicans, and sinners. To the respectable they were definitely bad company. He offered his friendship to anyone who needed it, but there were some people who shut themselves out. They were the people who loved and depended on power, the people who injured others, and those who thought themselves good. With these last he could do nothing. He even held out some hope – a slender hope – for rich people, but not for those who thought themselves better than their neighbours. They had locked themselves out of the Kingdom of Heaven. In the end he attacked the worst of these people – the Pharisees – with invective of the most passionate intensity.

Jesus would not allow anyone to call him good. He did not go to the publicans and sinners with an attitude of moral superiority; he went to them because he liked them, because they did not pretend to be anything but what they were, because they knew they needed him. He had compassion for them, he *felt with them*.

This may seem to some readers to have been a surprising digression on religion. But it was necessary, because I believe that only an understanding of religion will enable us to get beyond 'morals' to something that is not just a pattern of behaviour, but a way of life that will help us in the unusual and unexpected situations that we are all bound to meet.

There are many different approaches to religion. Some people undoubtedly reach its truth through what one might call the conventional approach. But many young men and women have been put off by what seems to them the arrogance of the claims of organized religion in the past and in the present. I would beg these young people to recognize that none of man's activities, individual or organized, are proof against evil. It is true that in certain sects and at certain periods much of the Christian Church's activity has been in no sense Christian. Very many of us who regard ourselves as members of the Christian Church are as well aware of this as are its bitterest critics. Religion has suffered radically from the activities of people who have taken their neuroses into it, people who instead of finding in it the answer to fear, cruelty, and meanness of spirit, have made of it a loathsome perversion – the very expression of hatred and sadism. They have turned Christianity into its opposite. I'm not thinking only of the Inquisition; of the Catholic, Protestant, and Calvinist brutalities, but also of the Puritan moralists whose attitude was a denial of the abundant life.

The fact that Christianity – seen in the understanding and daily living of humble people – has survived the terrible strain to which the Church has been subjected from within, is a testimony to the strength and truth of its original message. There are people in perhaps every section of the Christian Church who have got beyond quibbling about words and begun to discover what Jesus meant by the abundant life. Such people are not distinguished by the doctrines they accept but by the quality of their lives. They make one aware that the abundant life is a life lived very much in the physical world, using all our material and bodily resources and energy with as much insight and understanding of each other as is possible. It is not a vague ecstasy achieved during religious devotions, not a condition of spirit to be reached in the life to come; yet it in no sense depends on wordly success, power, or property. It is an everyday life lived richly, deeply, sensitively, and adventurously; and it can include in its wholeness, very significantly, the delights of sex.

16

ARE YOU IN A MESS?

WHAT should I say in this chapter? Perhaps this more than anything else: that this is not a book for good boys but for bad boys. That is to say that it is for everyone. Jesus, whatever you may think of him as a religious leader or of the religion that became based on his teaching, had a genius for seeing into men's hearts. He found the people of his time very much concerned with rules and regulations. The good people were those who kept the rules, the bad people were those who did not. The good people were very ready to accuse others of breaking the seventh commandment – the crime of adultery. But Jesus looked deeper and said to them: *Whosoever looketh on a woman to lust after her hath committed adultery with her already in his heart.* This has been too readily taken by humourlessly religious people to mean that we are all wicked men and that we ought never to want to go to bed with a woman until we have been through the marriage ceremony, that we ought never to find ourselves thinking, when in the company of an attractive woman: what would she be like to make love to?

Jesus was profoundly a realist; he knew exactly what men were like. It was his realism that gave him the confidence to deal so effectively with the men who brought to him the woman taken in the act of adultery, intending to stone her. *He that is without sin among you, let him cast the first stone.* He could be certain that every one of those men had either made use of a prostitute at some time or urgently wanted to. He gave the perfect answer, better than any moral arguments. *And they ... went out one by one, beginning at the eldest, even unto the last.*

So I think that Jesus, far from condemning us all for our thoughts and desires, accepted men and women for what they were and made it very clear that all shared the same

198

nature. Spiritually men could get nowhere unless they recognized this, recognized fully their kinship with each other, made no claims to perfection or to goodness. Yes, we are all in this together. Sex profoundly interests us all, and if it is bad to have sexual desires, thoughts, and temptations beyond what it is 'respectable' to have, then we are all bad boys, whether we are sixteen or sixty.

There isn't any doubt, however, that sexual desires lead some people into painful, even tragic, situations, while others through good fortune or wisdom are so fulfilled in their personal and sexual life that the control of wayward impulses becomes reasonably easy. Now what do I say to those who are in a mess? I'm not here concerned with those who are suffering from a broken-off love affair. It may be very painful but it is not a 'mess'; it is an experience through which you can get to know more about yourself and from which you can go on to something at least as good, if not better. It is a romantic and false notion that there is only one lovable person in the world. The more one knows of love, the more one becomes aware that there are very many lovable people in the world who would be a joy to live with. There is nothing really faithful about clinging to a memory. Life among people is endlessly interesting and stimulating, an adventure in which there is always more to be discovered, and never any lack of new territory! The pain of our early difficulties may make us more sensitive, capable of deeper joy and great satisfaction as we move on to new experience.

If you can't get free from bitterness, if you are tempted to cynicism, then you *are* in a mess. Something is wrong in you and what is wrong is not primarily sexual. Nothing should be allowed to cheapen our view of other human beings, or tempt us to make facile and disparaging remarks about the other sex. Not only do all men share the same nature, but all men and women. We are all capable of both triviality and nobility, of responding to others with meanness or generosity. We are all strung between good and evil and the only constructive thing to do is to accept each other in the deepest possible sympathy and compassion. Whenever anyone seems to fail us, we all in a sense share the responsibility for the failure.

Failure. What thoughts does that word evoke in you? A feeling of disgrace? An end? A situation in which you can do nothing? It is unfortunate that almost the whole of education is devoted to teaching children how to achieve success, hardly any of it to teaching them what to do with failure. If a boy or girl achieves success then his education has been worth while. If he or she fails, then the education is thought to have been – yes, *wasted* on him. That is putting the situation starkly, perhaps crudely, but it is in a very large measure true – and it is intended as a deep criticism of the motives that are encouraged in school. To be a scholar at a school that boasts a large number of 'successes' may be an unfortunate experience.

In fact, we all experience failure in a large measure. Success in business, or in gaining degrees, in climbing mountains, or in social eminence, is success in only one small aspect of a person's life. In some other respect everyone meets some degree of failure. This can be a tonic – a stimulating experience – or it can be simply failure, depressing and final, closing down one of life's activities. This depressing and frustrating result of failure is far too often found in people's sexual experiences.

What are the failures? All of us know of people who marry with great confidence but who before long are separated or divorced; we know of marriages coming to an unhappy end after many years of apparent normality; we know of unmarried mothers getting rid of their babies to an adoption home, or running away, leaving them in the maternity hospital; we know of young people irresponsibly indulging in intercourse and then one of them, often the girl, being 'shoved off' and suffering intensely; we know of boys punished for masturbation, even expelled in disgrace from school, and of others caught in homosexuality.

It is important, however, that we should not overestimate the sexual evil in the world. There are very many people who do not make a mess of their sexual relationships, who, even if their marriages are not specially creative, do maintain stable homes, bear their responsibilities gladly, and enjoy their children. In this book I have had to describe evils and underline actions that will lead to suffering, but it must be said that the human race has astonishing resilience, power of recovery, ability to survive disaster and failure. It is worth while to try to understand this resilience. Life is impossible without it and the more we have of it the better. A great deal of human resilience is unconscious; people are knocked down by disaster and rise up again undefeated simply because it is in their nature to do so. One of the deeply encouraging facts about the last war was the resilience of the ordinary people of London and other towns all over Europe under continuous bombing. It is in the nature of humanity to behave like this.

But we can do more. We can make this resilience conscious, we can increase our ability to survive and we can even make a failure a stepping-stone to greater maturity and deeper living. This is one of the central truths of Christianity. It is unfortunate that some of the religious moralists, tied to a hard-and-fast doctrine, have given the impression that if people behave properly they are inside the fold, 'saved', and if they behave improperly they are outside it. They forget the parable of the prodigal son. We are all of us in some measure prodigal sons.

Life can never be ideal. It can never be free from mistakes, crises, misunderstandings, quarrels, injustices, and unfairness. We can't escape these things by living to a pattern; life doesn't let us and people who try to live to a pattern become lifeless. But as we pass through these difficult experiences, we should try to control their effect upon us; to avoid becoming insensitive, casual, or embittered. The insensitive person develops a tough skin so that he shall not feel what has happened to him or to the other person; the casual – much the same type – slips out of situations apparently unaffected. The embittered man destroys his own life, and if he survives at all he does so twisted and maimed.

Perhaps the worst mess a young man may find himself in is the situation in which he has caused a girl to become pregnant, he has 'got her into trouble'. Now it is all too easy for an onlooker to preach to the sufferer, but all the same I can't help being aware from my observation of people that certain things are *true*. The first is that no good can come out of the situation unless you take some measure to the extent at least of saying: '*I* did this; now what?' The state of mind in which a man says: 'The woman tempted me...' solves nothing and may be cowardly even if it is true. The second truth is that if the man does take full responsibility there is a prospect of redeeming what may seem a desperately unfortunate experience. That is not to say that the practical consequences can be avoided; they have to be faced, intelligently, and generously dealt with.

What is the responsible way of meeting this situation? Our society, as you know, puts pressure on the couple to get married and make the girl respectable and the baby legitimate. In many instances the two people concerned would have married anyway and the ceremony is merely anticipated. Sometimes a couple who hitherto have carried on their relationship with each other at an extremely irresponsible level are sobered and matured by the experience and become able to make the beginnings of a responsible married life together, which may have some hope of settling into a permanent partnership, though probably they had no such intentions beforehand, and were concerned only with exploring the delights of physical sensation. But a marriage begun in this way needs a great deal of help if it is to develop into a lasting relationship of respect and mutual consideration. I do not believe that the couple in every instance should marry. The feeling of injury, for instance, may be irreparable, there may be no grounds for respect that can be built upon, the persons may be too young and immature to be thrust into the partnership of marriage with any hope of its holding together or coming to fruition in a good relationship. Those who have the responsibility of advising the young people should have other considerations in mind than the demand for regularizing a union and making it socially acceptable. If the young couple have either of them deep misgivings as to the suitability of their marriage in these circumstances, they should consult some responsible outside persons, such as members of the Marriage Guidance Council or ministers of religion who are known to be realistic and broadminded. The future of the baby the couple have called into the world should be a major consideration in their deliberations.

Sometimes the man is tempted to encourage the girl to have an abortion. I have already (Chapter 3) emphasized the serious dangers of this, especially if the girl attempts to cause an abortion by interfering with her own body or going to a 'quack' for an illegal operation. In other instances the girl deserts the baby in hospital or arranges for an immediate adoption. She may, however, keep the baby and bring it up, accepting all the responsibilities of motherhood, and trying to be its father too. It is difficult to believe that it is ever good for a girl to give up her baby and cut out all the normal experience of loving and nursing it. This is a tolerable procedure perhaps only if the girl is very young and hardly aware of what is happening to her. But if she keeps it and cares for it, how can the man behave responsibly other than by offering to marry her?

The very least he can do is to accept a generous share of the cost of maintaining the child right through its time of growing up. Beyond that, what can I say? No woman with self-respect wants a man to continue to visit her and the child as a *duty*; and if he feels more than a sense of duty, why not marriage?

There is another person to be considered as well as the girl. There is the child. 'Can't you get rid of it?' It! Is a baby a thing, just an object that has caused all the trouble? No reasonable man faced with that question will reply yes. Yet to many otherwise reasonable men, the baby in this troublesome situation becomes just a nuisance. And how the child pays for it! Much of the external stigma of illegitimacy has been removed in recent years and all the normal avenues of education and training are now open to the illegitimate. But this is not enough; from the moment a child is born he has a right to a normal home and parents.

This problem of the pregnant girl is so very different from most of the other problems in life that result from mistaken actions, and I am conscious of having made only a fumbling attempt to clarify it. But about one thing I can be definite – the need for far greater courage in men than is normally shown. It is in these affairs that we see men at their worst. Men do so much on land and sea and in the air to test out their physical courage, yet so often become cowards when faced with the consequence of 'a little bit of fun'. Men have such a code of 'sportsmanship' in their relations with each other, yet they can treat a woman, whom they have got into trouble, with such scant consideration and respect.

When we escape from the old idea of sex as sinful and dirty, it is possible to think of all sexual activity both within and without the moral code as potentially clean and innocent. But the irresponsible action, however 'innocent', still has its consequences. I know that there will continue to be many who have sex relations without marriage. To them I would say, at least be certain that you deeply love each other. When people really care for each other they have something that will enable them to deal with a situation constructively no matter how difficult, complicated, and unconventional it may be.

I ended the first chapter of this book with the question as to whether in all cases a satisfactory sex life requires that everyone should follow the conventional code. How do you think I have answered the question? I have avoided giving a definite yes or no, and I still avoid this, because it is one of those questions for which either of these answers would be misleading. I have wanted to encourage you to think about human relationships much more deeply than do most people who want quick answers, 'moral' or 'immoral'. I have tried to point a way out of the confusion in which many young people are caught. If you have read this book thoughtfully, your attitude of mind will have brought to the surface feelings and desires of which you were previously perhaps hardly conscious; and I believe that in most of you it will have aroused a desire to make something wholesome of your sex life and to avoid the mistakes and mess that you see around you. If I have aroused these feelings and set you thinking and feeling honestly, in time to avoid mistakes, I shall be glad.

But if you have made mistakes already, even though they may seem terrible and tragic, I want to end by reminding you that there are very few situations that cannot be redeemed and made good if the people concerned find the courage and honesty to begin again together, or with others, on a new basis of truth fortified by experience. We cannot escape from our past; it must be taken into the present and made use of.

There is one last point. The other day I heard a young woman say that she was going to buy a motor-cycle; there was no point in saving money if we were to be destroyed by a nuclear bomb before long. This was little more than a joke, but it occurred to me that perhaps many of the young people who plunge heedlessly into sexual experience are affected unconsciously, if not consciously, by the prevalent attitude of pessimism. 'Let's eat, drink, and have lots of sex, for tomorrow the hydrogen bomb!' Why save for tomorrow when tomorrow may never come?

We are all a bit affected by what appears to be the overwhelming threat of destruction. But to be morally defeated before it happens is unworthy of us as individuals or as a nation. I do not believe that civilization is going to be destroyed. Even if human organization is profoundly disrupted, human community will always be re-created, friendship will continue to make life worth while, and faith will give man the reason and the courage to build again, if he needs to. The human race has tremendous reserves of energy.

I do not say that we shall avoid suffering and disaster.

There is no easy time ahead – on the contrary perhaps the toughest trial the human race will ever have experienced. We need to be free in spirit if we are to give attention to what is required of us. We must not be bogged down in a nasty personal mess, sharing with the rest of our generation the hopelessness that results. The hydrogen bomb is not the invention of an evil power beyond our control; it was invented by men and it is within the power of men to abolish it. But only those who are free in spirit can get on with this task. Sexual experience that is ill-directed, distorted, turned in upon itself, is the great destroyer, whereas sex joyfully and wholesomely satisfied gives firm ground for faith in life and survival; it sets us free to think and act effectively.

INDEX